Praise for The Violet Shyness of Their Eyes: Notes From Nepal

Winner 1994 Pacific Northwest Booksellers Association Book Award

...well worth reading for the vivid description of what it is like for an aware American woman in her late forties to teach in Asia now.
— Women's Review of Books

[Scot's] reflections of this tiny, unspoiled land at the top of the world are often haunting. — New York Newsday

And while Scot never sugarcoats the hardships, she fulfills two of the travel writer's most important tasks: evoking a deep sense of place and instilling in the reader a desire to go there. — Booklist

Effectively, and more so, affectingly, Scot's notes from Nepal convey an American woman's journey out, beyond self, into self-knowledge.
— Small Press

...There is so much delicacy and warmth in this book! —Sipapu

...Scot's careful observation of Nepali culture gives the reader vivid snapshots of life in that developing country, while her careful self-observation yields a wealth of information about American culture.
— Seattle Times

This provocative book deserves attention from anyone interested in cross-cultural communication and the complex issues of development work.
— Yoga Journal

THE VIOLET SHYNESS OF THEIR EYES

NOTES FROM NEPAL

THE VIOLET SHYNESS OF THEIR EYES

NOTES FROM NEPAL

BARBARA J. SCOT

CALYX Books • Corvallis, Oregon

The publication of this book was supported with grants from the National Endowment for the Arts Literature and Advancement Programs, the Lannan Foundation, and the Oregon Arts Commission.

Cover photograph by Barbara J. Scot
Cover design by Cheryl McLean
Book design by Cheryl McLean and Micki Reaman

CALYX Books are distributed to the trade through **Consortium Book Sales and Distribution, Inc., St. Paul, MN, 1-800-283-3572.**

CALYX Books are also available through major library distributors, jobbers, and most small press distributors including Airlift, Bookpeople, Inland Book Company, Pacific Pipeline, and Small Press Distribution. For personal orders or other information write: CALYX Books, PO Box B, Corvallis, OR 97339, (503) 753-9384, FAX (503) 753-0515.

∞

The paper in this book meets the guidelines for permanence and durability of the Committee on Production Guidelines for Book Longevity of the Council on Library Resources and the minimum requirements of the American National Standard for the Permanence of Paper for Printed Library Materials Z38.48-1984.

Library of Congress Cataloging-in-Publication Data

Scot, Barbara J., 1942-
       The violet shyness of their eyes: notes from Nepal /
    Barbara J. Scot.
           p.   cm.
       ISBN 0-934971-36-6 (alk. paper): $24.95 --ISBN 0-934971-35-8 (pbk.): $14.95
       1. Nepal--Description and travel. 2. Scot, Barbara J., 1942-
    DS493.53.S36 1993
    915.49604--dc20   93-15123
                                                              CIP

Printed in the U.S.A.

9 8 7 6 5 4 3 2

ACKNOWLEDGEMENTS

Several people were instrumental in converting this personal experience into art. Jim Trusky, my husband, made the Nepal adventure possible with his love and support. My sons, Tim and Lon Murphy, were unwavering in their confidence that I could write a book. Maxine Trusky, my mother-in-law, read and re-read several drafts of the manuscript.

In addition to family members, several friends assisted me. Elly Branch, my running partner, for whom much of the manuscript was originally written in descriptive letters, listened to endless ruminations as I began to formulate the text. My dear childhood friend Lynn Balster Liontos read, edited, and corrected early drafts. Cheryl McLean, both a personal and professional friend, provided strategic focusing and editing which lifted the manuscript from personal reminiscing to a more universal plane. Ray Sherwood, my neighbor, whose afternoon walks in the park coincided with my writing breaks, listened patiently to emerging stories.

Educational compatriots were valuable as well. Earl Philips, longtime friend, gave essential technical assistance with computers because he believed in the importance of what I had to say. Tim Gillespie, a knowledgeable fellow writer, gave me the courage to continue by his faith in my bulky first draft and astute observations for improvement. Several readers—Bob Tidwell, Judy Woodward, Bert Trusky, Jan Engles, Chris Wills, and Roberta Cohen—made comments and gave encouragement that were essential.

I wish to pay special tribute to two friends. Dr. Charles Cannon, professor of English, Coe College, Cedar Rapids, Iowa, was willing, almost thirty years after he had coached me through his honors English class, to once again assume the role of mentor and advisor in writing for publication. His editing and his belief in my talent allowed me to believe in myself. Marilyn McDonald, counselor and educator with Reynolds High School, provided a continual source of inspiration for this work with her unflagging faith in the potential goodness of every person and her belief that each individual deserves dignity and respect. She is truly the sister of my soul.

And to the editors at CALYX—Micki Reaman, Cheryl McLean, Ann Mine, Beverly McFarland, Catherine Holdorf, Margarita Donnelly, and others—whose conviction in the value of nurturing the emerging woman artist has made possible so many fine works of art and whose creative, sensitive minds are part of this product we have finished together, I should like to say thank you. I feel fortunate and humble to have worked with you.

To Maxine Trusky
my mother-in-law

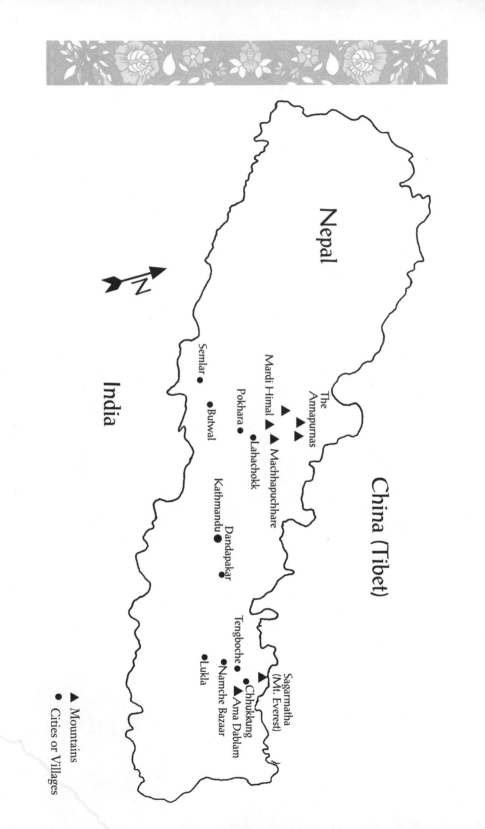

CONTENTS

I

ON THE ROAD TO KATHMANDU

A market vendor in Kathmandu

1

I was to regret that I did not heed the Nepali woman's demand to sit by the window. Enduring the nine or ten hours of fetid air in the crowded bus interior without even the benefit of daylight and with only an occasional gulp of wind was not an ordeal to which I would surrender willingly. *"Bujhina,"* I don't understand, I muttered, even though I knew almost every word she said. She continued to complain softly, and the four women who were crowded into the two seats in front of me rose and turned in unison to stare at the foreigner who was causing so much trouble. They were heavily decorated, with jewels in the center of their ears as well as the lobes, large ornaments in their left nostrils, and small gold rings through their septums. I hunkered down and looked out the window. The vendor beside the bus was selling tea, the glasses hastily dipped in the murky bucket beside him between customers. I would have liked some, but too recently had been sick to overcome my cultural fastidiousness about sanitation.

The massive peaks of the Annapurnas and the startling pyramid of Machhapuchhare were already catching the morning light. The choice in Nepal is to take a night bus or a day bus, but either way the rides are guaranteed to be lengthy commitments. They are not excursions undertaken for scenic pleasure as roads are dusty, rough, and frequently obstructed by landslides. The precipitous hillsides release gravel and boulders with monotonous regularity, a reminder that motorized vehicles are still intruders in Nepal. The first ever seen in the Pokhara River valley was a jeep brought in by plane in 1958.

When the bus was filled to a capacity that by any western definition would have been impossible, it lurched forward through the morning fog that was just beginning to lift from the lower river valley. The terraces were yellow or brown now, with the grain neatly piled in tufted stacks that squatted like giant toadstools in the fields. Much of the earth had been turned by the wooden plows. As the bus twisted laboriously up switchbacks, the Nepali women in front of me began to cough and spit out the window.

I'm not sure why Nepali women are so prone to motion sickness. Perhaps it is the infrequency with which they ride the bus. It could just be the stale, sweetish smell of too many bodies. Analyzing the cause of such an unpleasant sociological fact didn't interest me at that moment. I was feeling uncharitable. The wind from the open window carried unwelcome residue. I tried not to concentrate on the statistic from the medical lecture that each person with tuberculosis could infect forty-five others with one cough. Tuberculosis, once largely eliminated in the developed world, is a major health problem in Nepal. The woman beside me looked at me with misery in her large eyes. I would gladly have traded places then, but we were wedged in so tightly that change was not a possibility. The coughs progressed to genuine sickness, and the women leaned across each other to vomit out the window in a polite and orderly repetition.

The fog had cleared completely and the sun was warm through the glass. Men sitting on the other side of the produce-filled aisle removed towels they had wrapped around their heads against the predawn chill. The familiar noisy bus did not disturb the morning rhythms of hamlets through which it passed. In the sunshine, women sat on the low tile roofs patiently picking through each other's long black hair for lice. At each village tap, naked children were gathered, covered with soap as some patient elder, often a man, scrubbed the shivering brown bodies. Women bent over metal basins, kneading clothes, or knelt, scouring the black soot from pots with handfuls of sandy mud.

The narrow blacktop had long since changed to gravel. As the bus dipped closer to the river, it entered a long stretch of monsoon-damaged road. The repair project was a microcosm of developing nations at work. On the road a small yellow bulldozer labored back and forth with no apparent purpose. Beside the road scores of Nepali men attacked the large boulders with small picks. On a lower terrace beside the river, women sat pounding the rocks into gravel with larger stones or hammers. A red monkey on the other side of the water strolled along the sand with elaborate disinterest.

At Mugling the bus stopped and began to disgorge the tangled mass of bodies. It was time for morning *daal bhaat*, the staple meal of rice and lentils that is served twice a day. The small woman sat in a hump of misery between me and the path to the door. Nepali village women are very modest and rise before daylight to tend to their personal needs. On buses I have seen them avoid the admission of biological necessity that a trip to the public *chharpi*, toilet, would announce, and instead squat discreetly in the aisle while the men are outside. I gently moved her aside and squirmed out. I preferred a public *chharpi*, and I found one behind the *bhaat* shop. This shop served *maasu*, meat, with vegetables and rice. The freshness of the meat was evident—I picked my way through the chicken heads and blood to reach the *chharpi* by the river.

When the bus reloaded I would have liked to put the little woman by the window, but the order established at the beginning was inviolable for the rest of the trip. I climbed back to my seat and was soon cursing the fact that the women had eaten fruit taken from the folds of material around their waists and were repeating the cycle of illness. The one beside me pulled her *saari* over her head and used a plastic bag.

Finally the bus began to climb from the valley to the terraced hills again. The women in the seats in front of me slept in a tidy layering across each other, and the one beside me, who had sat for hours like a petite ghost under her *saari*, slumped against my shoulder in weariness. As the bus slowed and swung around a corner, her head wobbled. Whether she had given up all reserve or was sound asleep was impossible to say, with her *saari* covering her. Her head dropped to my lap.

She was no bigger than a child. I felt a rush of tenderness. All day I had resented her as if her misery had been privately aimed at me, but now, with her childlike warmth against my leg and the soft indiscriminate folds of her *saari* falling from her sleeping face, I felt deeply ashamed.

I was in a hard land by choice, seeking adventure, a self-imposed exile from a country where material comforts and economic prosperity were regarded as rights. This woman, for all the spectacular natural beauty of her surroundings and the pastoral simplicity of her existence—which I could idealize in letters home—experienced more *dukha*, more hardship, in a week than I would in a lifetime. Only for a moment was I privileged to understand something of the stoic courage required of the women in developing countries, and I had almost squandered it.

The bus continued interminably to climb. The sleeping woman's arm tightened unconsciously around my knee for steadiness on the switchback. The day was Mangsir 21, the year was 2047 in this Hindu nation, and it was at least two more hours to Kathmandu.

2

Usually, five of us go for tea. I am lucky to have so many women teachers at my school. Other western teachers are surprised when I tell them. I love the ritual of going for tea in the middle of the school day. One of the women always comes and rescues me from the language lesson with Indu, asking politely, "Madam, *chiyaa janne?*" Are you going to tea? So we go, *sabai*, all together, while the men teachers go to a different place. We stroll up the lane past a tethered buffalo to the *chiyaa* shop at the top of the hill.

They're gentle with me, even though I miss much of the conversation. I'm treated like a relative who is a bit odd, but loved, so included in family gatherings. Usually they talk of children or school, but sometimes they talk of me. Like yesterday. Shuku, who speaks the most English, didn't want me to be offended and asked, *"Bujhnu bhayo?"* Did you understand?

"Not all," I smiled, "but tell them I will NOT dye my hair black." They all laughed, for they had been discussing how it was strange that I was strong enough to climb a mountain when I had grey hair. Nepalis go to great lengths to keep their hair black.

They've been so nice to me that I finally feel brave enough to give something back, and today I have brought my photo album from home. I've shared a few pictures before, but never have I showed them the whole book. I wait until the *didi* has brought the tea before I pull it from my bag.

They are delighted. They all crowd around, including the *didi* and the other women who are with her in the shop. Two little girls, one who is in my fourth class and must belong to someone here, stand on the bench behind me to see.

"Mero shrimaan," my husband, I say, opening the book to a picture of Jim in a red coat. They smile delightedly, for they have seen a different picture of him before and recognize him. They say he looks like a Hindi movie star of some reknown because he has dark skin and a moustache. He also has black hair, which they like. They debate among themselves whether he is younger than I am, which I pretend not to understand. It would be highly unusual in Nepal for a woman to marry a man six years younger. I have my own cultural insecurities to deal with on that issue. In this picture Jim is fishing on the Metolius River in central Oregon, one of our favorite spots to camp.

"Maachhaa marnu," to fish, I explain. The phrase literally means to kill fish. They understand fishing. The lake Phewa Taal, in Pokhara, has fish. I decide to omit an explanation of Jim's catch-and-release philosophy. To hold food in your hand and voluntarily let it go would not translate well.

"Jetho chhora!" Oldest son, Laxmi exclaims at the next picture. She is right. But this picture causes great concern. It is an enlargement showing Tim climbing a rock pillar called Monkey Face at Smith Rock State Park in Oregon. It's a tall column which he assures me is not technically hard, but the exposure is impressive. The river is a silver snake far below him. He is swinging from a ledge called the Mouth Cave that is hundreds of feet from the ground as he continues the ascent to the top. The little girls cover their mouths in fright. *"Sanchai,"* he's fine, I try to assure them. He didn't fall. This is a sport. *"Kelna,"* game, is the closest I can come to the word. They shake their heads. Danger is not a game in Nepal.

"Kaanchho chhora!" Youngest son! They know Lon, too. But here he is dressed for his senior prom, standing beside Jim. We had gone to see his girlfriend's dress and her father had taken the picture. *"Bihaa?"* Wedding? No, I explain, *"Naach,"* dance. They like that. Nepalis love to dance. *"Dherai algo."* Lon is very tall. He looks nothing like Jim. They discuss this aberration.

"Mero saasu," my mother-in-law. They hum approvingly. Nepalis know all about *saasus.* They are important people in Nepal. I write my mother-in-law many letters. *"Raamro,"* good. One should

Women teachers at Byndabasini School, Pokhara

respect one's *saasu*. What amazes them is that my mother-in-law can read and write. My teacher friends are the first generation of Nepali women who have had access to education.

"Mero pariwaarmaa saat janaa chhan," there are seven in my family. It is a picture of our wedding, actually. There are the two of us, Jim's brother and his wife, and my mother-in-law. The kids are dressed in vests I made them, positively beaming with delight. I realize, with a start, we are standing in front of the American flag. The brief ceremony was in the courthouse in Vancouver, Washington. I do not mention it was our wedding as they have not been told I have been married twice. Divorce, which has only lately become legal in Nepal, is far from socially acceptable. Jim's brother looks like him. The teachers approve. I know they think we all live together and I do not correct them.

I turn the page to sudden embarrassment. The pictures are of marathons. In one I am standing with two women friends from home, and we are holding our trophies from a marathon relay. Our legs are bare! To my relief, my Nepali friends do not seem concerned. I am in another country in the picture. They are amused at the running. We translate twenty-six miles into kilometers. They laugh and mimic the running. But they marvel that I have *saathi*, friends, as crazy as I am.

Next the dogs, *kukur*. My two big white samoyeds are in several pictures. The women are curious. Most dogs are not pampered pets in Nepal. But one picture catches their attention. I have just brushed the biggest dog and a pile of white hair is beside her on the rug. I explain to Shuku, and she explains to the rest, that my friend makes weavings with the hair. *Raamro!* The affection lavished on the dogs is more understandable now.

Biraalo, cat. My little black cat named Prune perches on the closed toilet seat. They are not interested in Prune, but they are very interested in the oak toilet seat, which gleams a golden brown against the porcelain. I have never focused on its beauty at home. Finished wood is expensive and scarce in Nepal.

"Chhito, chhito," hurry, hurry, I say, for it is getting late. But they are not to be rushed. I turn to the last page. It is my backyard in full summer bloom. There are tubs of impatiens, mari-

golds, geraniums, and pots of mixed flowers. I love my yard in the summer. I told a friend before I left that it was tearing me apart to leave my flowers. My personality is a schizophrenic split between a constant yearning for adventure on one side and a deep satisfaction in tending my flowers on the other. Just to look at this picture could reduce me to homesick tears. My teacher friends begin to chatter excitedly. They point out familiar flowers to each other, giving them Nepali names. I am puzzled by their enthusiasm. I've not noticed much ornamental yard decoration in this land where every tillable inch of soil is needed.

I close the book, for it is time to go. They have accepted my gift and smile with warmth. They have enjoyed a brief glimpse into my other life, so far removed from theirs. The conversation continues and I can tell it is about *phul*, flowers, mine and theirs. On the way back to school, Laxmi motions me aside and points to her roof. For the first time I focus on the geranium pots up there, safely out of reach of grazing buffalo or goats. I smile and clap my hands in delight. Why is it that in Nepal where I was sent to teach, I always end up learning so much more?

I can hardly wait to walk home from school with my new eyes. It's such a thrill when this happens. Nepal has seemed at first such a random cultural tangle. But when I grasp a single strand and follow it, I am often surprised to find the root embedded in my heart. I skip out quickly after my last class. For the first time, I become aware that much of the beauty around me, which I have taken for granted in the colorful landscape of Nepal, is deliberately tended. Several roofs harbor geranium pots that are beginning, now that rains have come, to flower with color. A large clump of marigolds has a fence around it to keep it safe from livestock. And the orange trumpet vine curves in a trained arc over the wooden window frame of a house on Ram Krishna Tole.

*The Gurung family with whom Barbara
lived in Pokhara*

3

It's hard to get it just right in another culture. Our Gurung landlady and her family downstairs are so nice to us that Shelby, my young American housemate, and I have tried to do nice things for them, too. They always seem baffled at our gestures. Either we're uncertain they've understood or else we know for sure we've failed, like the time Shelby cooked a spaghetti dinner for them.

I should have warned her on that one, but I wasn't thinking straight either. We both knew how Nepalis are amazing in their singleminded loyalty to *daal bhaat*. Shelby loves to have people for dinner and I hate it, so I didn't want to be objecting again and didn't voice my apprehensions strongly enough.

Sure enough, the only thing that got eaten was the popcorn served before the meal. Nepalis often serve that. The spaghetti was shoved into pathetic little piles, and it hunkered down apologetically on the plates. Shelby was sad and felt like a failure even though I gave an encouraging pep talk about cultural differences and assured her it was excellent spaghetti, which it was. But last week I finally got it right with the honey.

Saturday morning I was here alone. It was quite early when I heard someone on the porch. I hadn't put the latch on after I came back from my morning run, which I usually do if I'm around home. I have never fully adjusted to the Nepali custom of walking in unannounced. Besides, now that it's warmer, I often wear shorts inside, which is not decent attire here. I don't want to offend anyone, even on what I consider to be my own turf. I came out in the hallway, luckily fully clothed, and right outside the screen door was a diminutive man in village Gurung attire, grey-brown tunic and shorts, looking like something out of *National Geographic*. (The November 1988 issue, to be precise. I've just looked it up in the pile Shelby has here.) *"Ouu, didi,"* oh, sister, he called softly.

I went out on the porch. He didn't say anything, assuming correctly I wouldn't understand Gurung at all and that my Nepali was limited. *"Hajur?"* I responded, and he showed me a large plastic jug wrapped in a cloth of questionable sanitation. It took careful inspection to figure out that what he was selling was honey. I was delighted. And then I recognized his appearance. He looked exactly like a picture in *Honey Hunters of Nepal*, the book I'd been perusing in Kathmandu the previous weekend.

"Exchen," one minute, I said, as it was obvious I needed my own container. I went back in the kitchen and got a plastic peanut butter jar. *"Kati rupia?"* How many rupees, I asked.

He squinted and held the jar at arm's length. *"Ek saya,"* one hundred, he said.

"Dherai mahango!" Too expensive, I exclaimed, as that is expensive indeed for anything to eat in Nepal. He held out the jar again. Ninety. Well, okay, it's not every day a man steps out of *National Geographic* to sell you honey.

He filled the jar carefully and I went back inside to get the money. Now here was the problem. I had a fifty rupee note, a twenty, and a five hundred. Surely he couldn't change the five hundred. I did a quick pocket search to no avail, then went back out on the porch with the money to try to explain the situation. Of course he didn't have change. I offered to pour some back in the jug for seventy rupees, but he didn't want that. He offered to sell me the big jug for six hundred rupees, which would have been quite a bargain. This was all done by gestures and with minimal Nepali. I didn't want the big jug, as the peanut butter jar alone was beyond my needs.

He sighed, and took the five hundred note, signaling he would go and get change. I was suddenly apprehensive. You will return, I asked in Nepali. He stared at me with wounded dignity and then set the big jug beside me and disappeared down the steps.

He was gone a long time. I began to think I had acquired a huge hoard of honey. I probably shouldn't have bought any honey at all, as no matter how tightly contained it was, it could draw ants. Shelby had just ingeniously conquered the ants before she left for vacation by stuffing insect-repellant-soaked cloths in the cracks under doors and windows. Any ants that returned would be solely attributable to me. And he probably hadn't expected to get that many rupees anyway. I was no doubt being charged a *bedeshi*, foreigner, price. That was the last money I had for the month. I glared at the dirty honey jug. I'm such a sucker for anything picturesque.

But he came back. Just when the sun was starting to hit the porch and I'd shifted the jug over into the shade, I heard the latch on the gate. I suppose he'd had trouble finding change because it was still so early. He gave me four hundred ten rupees in ridiculously small notes, handing it to me to count.

Then I had an idea. *"Exchen,"* one minute, I said. I went inside and got another jar. *"Arko,"* another, I said, *"mero pariwaar kolaagi,"* for my family, pointing downstairs. His brown face creased in a smile. He poured it carefully. I counted out ninety more rupees. Then I added ten more. He smiled again, saluted me politely, and was gone.

I took the jars inside and carefully washed them so there would be nothing to attract ants. The jars were full to the top. I took a spoonful from one. The honey, thick and dark amber, was smooth and rich. I don't know from which blossoms it comes, but according to the book, the bees who make it *(apis laboriosa)* are the world's largest honeybees, and the men who gather it rappel over steep cliffs on vine ropes.

When the jars were dry I placed one in the heavy saucepan with the lid, where surely no ants would notice, and I took the other one downstairs. *"Namaste,"* I called the polite greeting through the door.

"Aunuus," come in, replied the *hajaraamaa*, grandmother, but I waited outside, because to enter was to surrender to tea and conversation and I had work I wanted to get done. She came to the door and held it open. She is my favorite of them all, her back permanently bent from all those years of carrying wood in the village.

"*Tappai kolaagi,*" for you, I said. She looked at me, puzzled, when I held out the jar. I took off the lid and held it out, repeating that it was for her. Suddenly she understood that it was honey. She pressed her palms together and touched her forehead with her hands. She reached for it, then turned and smiled. She brought her hands, this time with the jar, to her forehead again. I raised my hands as well.

"*Namaskaar,*" I said, using the most respectful form, before I turned and went upstairs. I was surprised at the tightness in my throat. When I reached the kitchen, I saluted the saucepan that held my jar of honey. "Thank you," I said, and then I twirled around the room. It felt so good to know, at last, that I had done something for them that I knew for sure was right.

Gurung grandmother, Pokhara

II

IN ANOTHER COUNTRY

Sunlight in the mountains north of Pokhara

The Columbia Gorge that widens onto the plain on which I live in Portland, Oregon, and the Pokhara Valley in which I lived in Nepal are both the geological result of catastrophic floods. Large dams built from ice and earthen debris in high mountains collapsed, releasing torrential outpourings that carved new geographical features on the topography.

Mine is not a particularly teleological view of the universe in relation to either natural or human events, but I was early inculcated with Biblical imagery. I have seen rainbows arching against both Mt. Hood in Oregon and the Annapurnas in Nepal, so I can easily imagine that as the cataclysms subsided, the light was refracted through watery prisms, giving brilliant color to landscapes that were dramatically changed. The fractured dam, the ensuing flood, and the crystal prism constitute my metaphors for this work. On a humble human scale I re-enacted this drama. In my country we call this a mid-life crisis.

One morning in February of 1990 in Portland, I woke early with a headache so blinding that I had to feel my way to the bathroom. After I had been violently sick, I called the substitute teacher number and staggered to the couch. At first the pain was such that I could not lie down. As it lessened I fell into a restless sleep, still sitting up. Fragmented and confused images from my life tumbled kaleidoscopically through my dreams. When I finally awoke the pain was gone. I knew with a frightening clarity that I would have to leave. I did not know where I would go, how long I would be gone, or if I would ever come back. But I knew a door in my mind had opened and if I refused to leave the safety of the inner room, I would begin to die. I was able to lie down then, and I slept deeply for several hours. By September I was in Nepal.

The dam had burst. I did not yet know the debris of my past that would come tumbling over me in such dislocated circumstances. Nor did I know the beautiful colors that would be possible with life refracted through the prism of Nepal.

1

Kathmandu
September

Yesterday the American trainees sat in stunned silence through the official demonstration of how one uses the *chharpi*, squat toilet. A small Nepali man, with a perfectly straight face, got up in front of the group, placed two bricks on the floor, and squatted with a foot on each brick. He went through the appropriate facial contortions to make sure we understood. Dipping his left hand in an imaginary bucket of water, he wiped himself. After he feigned pulling up his pants, he went to another bucket with soap and washed his hand carefully. He then dumped the last bucket of water down an imaginary hole.

After the *chharpi* demonstration we listened to a lecture on the various forms of diarrhea we could expect to encounter. This topic, with good reason, is a preoccupation of westerners' conversations here. Kathmandu has some of the dirtiest water in the world. From one sip the following effects are possible in one to ninety days: salmonella, toxiogenic ecola, shigella, giardia, amoebas, worms, and hepatitis. The average development worker submits thirty-eight stool samples to the medical center in the two-year term of service.

Tomorrow we leave for a village, Dandapakar, and I'm glad it is at a higher elevation. September is still uncomfortably hot and steamy in Kathmandu. We have arrived prior to the major festival of Dasaai, a nine-day celebration. That schizophrenic split with which I always encounter newness already invades my perceptions. Part of me trembles with excitement as I walk through this strange and beautiful city, which is so filled with colorful squalor. But the other part of my mind longs for the autumn coolness in Oregon and the green quiet of the Mt. Hood cabin where the red vine-maple leaves arch over the creek.

▲

Dandapakar
September

I am sitting for a minute on the low stone wall behind the compound to watch the sun set behind the purple terraced fields that fall in an endless cascade into the valley. In truth, I don't know why I had to come to Nepal.

Yet I know when this journey began. The summer after Tim graduated from high school, he insisted on riding his bike over the Cascades to a science camp in eastern Oregon. As I sat on the backyard deck watching him pack, I resisted the urge to tell him he would never make it to the cabin by dark. The little boy in my mind had somehow turned into a slender young man. His serious face looked quite mature in the slanting rays of the afternoon sun. Then, abruptly, he was gone. I sat on the deck looking into the park. Two small blond boys were playing on the slide. Only a few years ago they would have been Tim and Lon. The ice cream wagon with its haunting circus song came up the street. The small blond boys ran across the grass. How many times had I watched that scene? Now the summers of swimming lessons, backyard Shakespeare, and family bike trips were done. But the faint wind that made cool lines down my cheeks also lifted my hair. I felt an unexpected stirring of freedom and restlessness.

▲

Today I got up at 5:30, as soon as it was light, with the intention of running as far as I could. I have been able to run almost every morning, although I have to wear long pants. The women of the village, who stared in surprise the first day I ran, ignore me now. They seem to have far too much work to be concerned with the crazy foreigner.

When I started running, the green rugged mountains glowed softly and white mist hung in the folds of the valleys. Children were already playing on the huge bamboo swings especially constructed for the Dasaai holiday. Clusters of men and women surrounded long poles that were bent and tied to a center point with vines. I ran past the prayer flags and village houses where radios blared music in honor of the holiday, past the small Buddhist shrines called *chortens*. After forty-five minutes of climbing a fairly steep grade, I left the road and followed a trail to a break in the rocks. I stepped through the cleft to a postcard view of Nepal. White mountains with shining snowfields stretched endlessly across the northern skyline. The sun split in long shafts over the green ridge in the east.

▲

The grain terraces that cover the slopes catch the sinking sun, and across the valley houses group in cozy clusters. No roads lead to these villages. Only footpaths connect them. Below me a man follows the water buffalo with a wooden plow.

A woman with a fodder-filled basket on her back labors up a distant hill. Great physical strength is demanded of these women whose beauty is positively startling. They are slight of build with violet eyes. Their hair is black and long, their skin all glowing shades of brown. I am an awkward giant beside them, with clumsy hands and feet.

The sun has melted in a golden pool behind the ridge. The steep hills fade to blueness in the last light.

▲

We sit on the floor for meals. We are given *daal bhaat*, rice accompanied with lentil soup and cooked vegetables, twice a day, the Nepali custom. The soupy *daal* and vegetables are mixed by the fingers with the rice and eaten with the right hand. There are no utensils. A sweet milky tea is served in glasses.

For six hours a day we study language. I am one of the slower students. Although the Nepali language trainers are soft-spoken and gentle, I am embarrassed by my difficulties. "You are old," the young trainer said sympathetically, in an effort to reassure me that I would ultimately be successful. I was not comforted by his remark. Life expectancy in Nepal is forty-three.

At night I study long lists of words by flashlight. Often the erratic electricity supply shuts down. The wires only extend along the road, so the lights I see across the valley must be fires or lanterns.

▲

If I have the time right, on the other side of the world Jim should be just getting ready for the marathon.

"*Bihaa bhayo?*" The language trainer asks me.

"*Bhayo,*" I answer. That means I am married.

Then the trainer says, "*Tapaaiko shrimaan naam ke ho?*" What is your husband's name?

"Jim," I say. "*Mero shrimaanko naam* Jim *ho.*"

How I long now for the less complicated anxiety of the early marathon morning instead of the loneliness I am feeling tonight. I would know, then, that by noon the ordeal would be finished with its definite measure of success or failure. Twenty-six miles seems a comfortable, definable distance.

I can hear rats gnawing in the ceiling at night. I whisper my name over and over. For the first time since we were married, I wish I had changed my name to Jim's so the recitation in the night would link me to him. As it is, I only feel more alone.

▲

The festival of Dasaai finally ended. On the ninth day, much to my horror, the Nepali trainers led away the pigmy goats that I had found so charming as they leaped from level to level in the compound. Bhumi, the chief language trainer, who is the oldest male and a Brahmin, ceremoniously chopped off a goat's head and smeared the blood on the agency van. I was told this by the others, as I chose not to watch. The goat meat was served with evening *bhaat.* I held to my vegetarian stance. *Maasu kandina.* I don't eat meat. My lie of convenience is becoming a sincere conviction. I will miss the friendly goats.

Cows, however, are safe from meeting the goats' fate. Cows are sacred in Nepal for they lead souls to heaven. One would be jailed for killing a cow. I am told with some disgust by a Nepali language trainer that not only do the Muslims eat a cow after it has died, but some of them are suspected of helping the cows along the way to death. In what contempt would she hold me if she knew my childhood?

A large truck was backed up to the side of the barn when I came home from school on the yellow bus. Strange men were loading the steers, using long prods with electricity. We rode all night to Chicago with my Uncle Jim, sleeping in the car. The next day at the stockyards a fat man gave Uncle Jim a check for a large sum of money. We gasped when he showed us. Then he took us to see where the cattle died in rows, hanging by their hind legs.

▲

Everywhere I have seen fathers carrying children. Often one is scrubbing a child at the water tap with gentle ease. I am touched by the obvious familiarity of men with tasks of childcare. Today I walked through the village in the late afternoon. On the open porch of a small house a young father squatted, rocking the baby in his arms and singing. His dainty wife knelt beside them, tossing rice rhythmically. The rice snapped against the flat circular straw disc she swung in graceful arcs.

When I was very small, my mother rocked me in the old wicker chair and sang to me before I went to bed. In the summer long shafts of light came through the golden brown window in the west. "Baby's boat's a silver moon..." I knew what that meant. It meant the new moon was curved like a heavy-sided hoop, and up above you could see the rim of the old moon. "Far across the sea..." The sea was what was in the Peter Pan book where the lost boys and Wendy were in the boat and the picture was full of clouds and swirls. "Only don't forget to sail..." My mother's voice broke a little. "...back again to me..." It had to do with my daddy. The song started again. The wicker squeaked rhythmically and where the weave was broken, it pressed against my leg. I could not bear to hear the sad part again. Stop, Mama, my leg hurts.

Perhaps they were right, those literature professors in college, that the search for the father would dominate western psychological themes of the twentieth century. But surely not in Nepal. "And when my father returns," the language trainer said today, "my mother will bow and touch her forehead to his feet."

Nepali father and children

2

Dandapakar
October

Today is the third day of the festival of Tihaar. I asked Sapana, the language trainer who shares my sleeping quarters, what we were celebrating this time. Should I read about it so I would understand? She laughed. "We don't have to understand to celebrate," she said. I persisted, feeling I should be a responsible student. So she summarized the activities, concluding, "Love. And brothers. It's about loving and honoring your brothers."

The first day was the day of the crow, which is the messenger of the god of death. Food was put out for the birds. The second day honored the dog, the guardian of the realm of the dead. Everywhere dogs wore garlands of flowers around their necks and *tika*, red rice paste, on their foreheads. Today, cows, which lead souls to the final state of nirvana, the release from reincarnation, sported wreaths of flowers and red *tika*. Tomorrow the celebration will honor the bullocks, which plow the fields. The last day all the sisters give their brothers presents of appreciation. If a husband is not forthcoming, the girls will be protected by their brothers.

I try to picture my brother infirm and old, as my ex-sister-in-law described him in her letter that came today. We were so close in childhood, as children are when no one else is there. How I envied him then, for he was the boy and I was only a girl.

I think of him in the words of the letter. The white hair is not hard to imagine, as that is hereditary, and mine is white as well. But the wheelchair, the cane, the virtual inability to navigate on his own is difficult for me to fathom. He is only two years older than I.

I have not heard from him in almost fifteen years. At times I was sure that he was dead. After guilty dreams, I started the Salvation Army on a fruitless search.

Strange that this letter should finally come when I am again a child in understanding the culture that surrounds me. I am quiet and do as the trainers tell me. I accept their explanations as truth. And here, again, my little girl eyes have quickly perceived that the boys are most valued. The trainers say that in villages where food is scarce, the little girls are often malnourished, for they are the last to be fed.

▲

Today Bishnu Bhandari of Tribhuvan University came all the way to Dandapakar to address the American trainees. His topic was described in the syllabus as "Development and Nepal." I was relieved to have a brief reprieve from the intense language training. I enjoyed listening to a lecture in English, although some of what he said was disquieting.

Bishnu Bhandari said that when he was a child, his mother spent more than three hours a day getting water. Now a water tap stands in the center of the village. Today, almost all of the twenty-nine thousand villages in this land of eighteen million people have some form of running water. So some aspects of development have been good. "We have done so many things, just in my lifetime," he said. When he went to high school, he had to walk a whole day from his village. For college, he walked three days to a road where he could get a ride on a truck to Kathmandu. Although his village is now served by a road, many places in Nepal still exist in this kind of isolation.

Bishnu Bhandari's father did not know about World War II until three years after it ended. Now every village has a battery-operated radio. If war breaks out in the Middle East, all of Nepal will know the very day it happens.

But Bhandari suggested that development has changed Nepal in negative ways as well. Theft and robbery have become common. Suicides were virtually unheard of until recently. Marijuana, which was used before the coming of foreigners in a limited, traditional way, has become a commercial enterprise. Addictive drugs such as heroin and cocaine, introduced by westerners in the 1970s, are now imported illegally from Thailand and Pakistan.

What Nepal needs, according to Bishnu Bhandari, is sustainable development. "We must be self-reliant. We must give priority to agriculture and raise productivity. We must increase our hydroelectric power. We must encourage small tourism because the large tours who stay in five-star hotels eat only imported food and contribute nothing to the economy. We must think small scale. Ninety-one percent of the Nepali population is still involved in agriculture. Each family tills an average of 1.5 acres."

I found this man fascinating. I waited to see what he would say about education to a group who had been sent by a foreign government to help in the schools. He did not mention the schools directly, but what he said about language is this: Almost fifty languages exist in Nepal. In an effort to establish uniformity in the schools, each child is required to learn Nepali as the language in which the lessons are presented. When the children speak only the Nepali language in the schools, they experience one loss. As they learn English, they experience another. The problem, he said, is that the cultural meaning of words is so much richer than the translation. To say *aamaa* is to say so much more than mother. There is no explanation for the meaning of *aamaa* in English. "We are losing our own traditions," he said.

I do not know all the meanings of *aamaa* in Nepali and I do not like to feel that I will play a part in a loss of traditions. But I do know that in any language the meaning of mother is so much more than the word.

I loved her with the painful intensity that develops in children when they realize their very existence is what gives life meaning to a parent whose other dreams have gone awry. Mine was a lonely prairie childhood with long farmhouse windows staring blankly at the open spaces. My mother taught me to look for beauty in sudden unexpected places and gave me images to catch it in—lightning that ripped the sky in eggshell pieces or silver maple leaves with their souls turned inside out before the rain.

Then suddenly she was gone. I had no idea what to say to the familiar people who sought to comfort me with euphemistic phrases that for me no longer bore any relation to reality. They seemed to be saying the most childlike things that threatened to invalidate my grief. The hand that I had touched was very cold.

3

Butwal
October

We left the village of Dandapakar after six weeks of intensive
language and cultural training during which the trainees were
mostly sequestered in a small compound of cement huts. Next,
we stayed briefly in Kathmandu. There we received another round
of innoculations intended to make us immune to a variety of the
medical problems that are routine for the Nepalis. Perhaps this
is a comfortable fiction, as one American was just diagnosed with
hepatitis.

Yesterday we rode several hours on the bus to Butwal for the
next phase of training, which will last about four weeks. The language classes will continue, but part of the day will be devoted to
learning about education. Each trainee will live with a Nepali family
during this month. Butwal is a medium-sized city approximately
thirty miles north of the Indian border. Directly behind the town
begins the *pahaad*, the green foothills of the Himalayas. The city
itself sprawls along a river in a curious assortment of low buildings.

The atmosphere differs startlingly from Dandapakar, where life
moved quietly and sounds disappeared in the blue mist between
the steep valleys. Noises quiver as if trapped in the dusty heat that
hovers over Butwal. Perhaps the abrupt wall of the *pahaad* simply sends the sound waves back over us. All the people appear to
be engaged in noisy commerce. Rickshaw drivers with turbans on
their heads shout to each other. Water buffalo and small oxen
pull wooden-wheeled carts. Brindled cows with humps and calm
eyes stand in the middle of the road. Stacks of brass water urns,
gaudy fabrics, and women's make-up from India fill the shops.

In Butwal I have already gained much more of a sense of the political revolution happening in Nepal. Last night a noisy torchlight parade of Communists thronged through the streets. They demanded a new constitution that would grant more rights to the people. Until recently, the people of Nepal revered their king as a manifestation of one of the gods. But in the last few decades the political climate has begun to reflect the infusion of competing ideologies from India and China. Last spring over five hundred people were killed when forces representing change united for large demonstrations. These turned into confrontations with the military, which is loyal to the king. This violence, common in many Asian countries, was shocking in Nepal, with its tradition of peaceful tolerance. The king, acting on advice to moderate his powers before it was too late to salvage the existing structure, agreed to issue a new constitution. The promised date for this concession recently passed. The Americans are here at the invitation of the king, so we are encouraged—in fact required—to remain completely neutral politically.

We spent last night on the floor of the school, but tomorrow we will move in with our homestay families. This school complex, a training center for Nepali teachers, includes two large buildings, unoccupied at the moment. At first I thought the Nepali teachers must be on vacation, but today I heard that the training programs shut down for lack of money. Nepal has, we have been told, enough trained teachers, so many, in fact, that some are without jobs. The Americans have been imported as "foreign experts" to help Nepali teachers improve their teaching techniques. The first year of the assignment each volunteer is assigned classes in a particular school. This is to familiarize the volunteer with the educational system in Nepal. Does it also mean a Nepali teacher is unemployed, I asked Sapana, for we had been discussing the difficulty of teachers securing positions. The competition for employment as a language trainer had been fierce, she told me, with hundreds of applicants for thirty positions. She did not look at me to answer, for she knew the implication of my question.

"Yes," she said finally. "It probably means that."

I am increasingly baffled. In the second year of the assignment the volunteers are to run workshops for veteran Nepali teachers to help them improve methods of instruction. Yet only three of the thirty-five American trainees have teaching credentials or have spent any time in the classroom. At home they would not even be allowed to teach. They certainly would not be asked to train teachers. My questions about this to either American or Nepali trainers elicit only vague replies.

▲

Today our homestay families arrived to claim us. My *aamaa*, mother, who in my case is really my *bahini*, younger sister, was bursting with pride. She rented a rickshaw to carry us through the business district, all the way to the edge of town.

When we arrived in front of the house, the *aamaa* dismissed the rickshaw driver with a few *rupia* and an imperious toss of her head. She led me toward the house. Neighbors, young and old alike, gravitated into the small yard and surrounded me completely. My attraction has persisted now for two hours. I quickly exhausted all the Nepali words I knew and now am reduced to nodding and smiling. My grey hair and the gold in my teeth attracted special interest from the beginning, and the ones standing nearby still point into my mouth for the newcomers. Finally, tired and confused, I managed to convey that I would like to rest. No less than ten people have crowded into the little room with me where I am told I will sleep with the youngest daughter. Several are bending over the bed to pick up my things and set them down carefully. In desperation for privacy, I have begun to write, which they observe with interest.

▲

Nepalis do not knock before they enter closed doors as it is assumed one will always be decently covered. I suppress a wave of indignation when someone bursts in unannounced. This whole experience is a challenge to the right of privacy we assume at home. In Nepal the need to be alone would be culturally aberrant and usually physically impossible. I think with some amusement now of the festering family argument that occasionally resurfaced because each of my sons felt entitled to a room of his own.

The area that the boys resented sharing was approximately the same size as the house in which I am residing in Butwal. I can't even figure out how many people live in this odd conglomeration of tiny rooms. Wooden slat beds, covered with bamboo mats, inhabit every conceivable nook and cranny. At night a variety of people occupy the beds, sometimes two or three to the same set of slats. Behind the main house a makeshift dwelling squats by the water tap. It houses several more people who seem vaguely related to the main family here. Some disappear during the day and reappear toward evening, so they may be workers or servants. The *aamaa*, mother, refers to two of the women as *bahini*, little sister, but the term is used to establish age relationship as well as biological ties. In Nepal, everyone is family.

One room in the main house holds a TV and a VCR, which are neighborhood attractions when the electricity is working. In the evening the outer fringe of the dwellers here, as well as assorted neighbors, spend an hour or two leaning over each other's backs at the window to see the Hindi programs broadcast from India. I am straining not to be judgemental concerning the choices of modernization in this household.

A communal *chharpi* leans against the makeshift dwelling by the water tap, but the *aamaa* is embarrassed to have me use it. In fact, she did not respond to my repeated questions about its location and I had to discover it by stealth. She arranged with a little school next door for me to use their toilet between the hours of 8 a.m. and 8 p.m. Nature calls at night result in furtive trips to the garden.

All night long a hot wind blows off the plains that stretch up from India. It swirls unimpeded through the cloth covering over the tiny window by my bed. Dust rises from the packed dirt floor. I coat myself with insect repellent to keep off fleas and mosquitos, a losing battle. The crowd that sleeps outside pull their *lungis*, loose all-purpose cloths that serve as wraps, over their faces to sleep.

Is privacy, which we regard so fiercely as our due at home, merely a luxury of wealth and sparse population? Have I accepted as an inalienable human right something which may be only a culturally specific habit of a certain time and place?

▲

A new goat, black and white with gentle eyes, stood tied to the stake in front of the house last night. He moved restlessly, though. He might have known that a Nepali picnic wouldn't be a treat for him.

When the American trainees and their host families got on the bus in the morning, the goat was loaded, too, and stood quietly in the aisle. The children were wildly excited, and the three little girls in front of my seat rode backwards to stare at the white foreigners. One had a thorn through her left nostril where it had just been pierced for a jewel. We answered their questions in broken Nepali. They chattered happily as we passed thatched huts with melons growing on the roofs.

When we got to the spot by the river we all got off the bus, including the goat, and unloaded huge pots, sacks of rice, and vegetables from the roof rack. Then the women, sitting on the bamboo mats that were spread out on the grass, began cutting up the vegetables and tossing the rice. The men gathered wood and sharpened the knife.

In Nepal one of the signs of manhood is to be able to cut off the head of an animal with one stroke. One man sprinkled water on the goat, which stood quietly, as another man raised the knife. I didn't watch that part but the cheer meant it had been a good clean cut. Then they scraped the hair with flat knives and cut the meat in stew-sized hunks.

Next they began to dance. First the Americans had to dance, a token gesture, because the Nepalis are the ones who really wanted to dance. They had rigged up a sound system with a car battery, but it broke down so they went back to their drums and sang. The children danced one by one, then men danced with men. The drums and singing went on and on with the women dancing, sometimes singly and sometimes in groups but never with the men. All during the festivities an old woman lay on a bamboo mat, moaning softly. When I asked what was wrong, my *aamaa* told me that the woman's son had recently died. Different women went to sit with her. She was not alone all day.

The meal was served on plates made of saal leaves sewn together.

Women preparing vegetables for
a picnic near Butwal

We ate, using the fingers of our right hands. Huge mounds of rice accompanied by soupy *daal*, the cooked vegetables, and the goat meat constituted the main meal. For dessert, the women served a special treat, a sour yogurt with pineapple and bananas.

After the meal the pots and pans were scrubbed with sand in the river. I tried not to notice the children squatting upstream. My *aamaa* drank the water from her hand.

They danced until the sun went down. Then we went back to the bus—which even without the goat was filled to overflowing. I rode on the bus top with several Nepalis. A full moon came up over the hills by Butwal. All the way back the Nepalis sang, and a young man danced on the roof of the bus until he fell across the others' laps.

▲

My luck with good health finally ran out, and yesterday I came down with a fever, *wok-wok* and *disaa laagyo*—that's vomiting and diarrhea—under humiliating conditions. The good thing is that I am now in the training quarters under a mosquito net and a fan. For the first time in Nepal, I have a door I can close, and people knock before they enter. The medical culture shows worms and amoebic dysentery. I am running a troublesome fever. I have slept for hours, which may be from the relief of a little privacy more than from the severity of the illness.

I try to rouse myself for I know it is a dream, but each time my mind slips back into it again. I am tangled in a spider web of white net. I drink the boiled water that has been left by my bed. Then I am back in the dream. I am sweating, but I am very cold.

When my brother and I were very young, we both slept between flannel sheets in the west room in the winter. Our mother would heat the water for the water bottles. We would curl around the water bottles, which were hot, while the air outside the covers was like ice. Well into the night we would play the Game. It was a dialogue that involved a large imaginary family with a father. No one knew of the game but us, but our mother would come, finally, hearing our voices, and tell us to go to sleep.

We played the game for years. It was an ongoing dialogue. I do not remember that we ever talked of real happenings or people to each other.

Certainly we did not talk of our real father. Our imaginary father was always there, although he was stern. He was often angry with our pretend sister, but never with us. I was a boy in the game, as I desperately wished to be in real life. Our sister did not behave as well as we boys did. We were strong and brave and defended the livestock from dangerous predators.

In early adolescence I wanted out of the game, but my brother persisted for a long time. I can see him, standing at the foot of my bed in the south room, weaving a long monologue to which I refused, uncomfortably, to respond. I felt disloyal when he finally left the room.

In the Army the drinking started. First, the denial, the long silences, the financial problems and vague conversations that were as far from reality as our childhood game. The rest is hazy, anybody's alcoholic relative. And then I lost him completely.

But the dreams started. And always he was standing at the foot of the south room bed, trying to weave the web of dialogue, but I was refusing to respond.

Twice my brother has been here tonight, standing at the foot of the bed. But I am in another country. I cannot be my brother's keeper here.

How hard this is! To try to live in another society on its own terms is to lose all the adult advantage of control. I had to be taught again how to eat and eliminate waste. I can neither read nor write. At times I know those around me are discussing me, but I do not catch all the words. And to make it worse, my dreams are a confusion of scenes from my own childhood and the childhoods of my sons. I no longer know whether I am the mother or the child.

III

CHHORI CHHAINA?
(YOU HAVE NO DAUGHTERS?)

Ox cart at sunset, Semlar

1

Semlar
November

I am in a little village called Semlar that looks like something from my sixth-grade geography book. I arrived a week ago and will remain for a month, practicing my teaching skills and language in the village school. My sleeping quarters are an empty room rented from a local family, and my meals have been arranged at the village *bhaat* shop. Semlar must be situated thirty miles or so west of Butwal in the Terai, the thin, flat strip of land that is between the Indian border and the first dramatic rise of the foothills of the Himalayas. No doubt the temperature is intolerably hot in the summer, but it is bearable now, in the high eighties during the day. The nights cool down nicely. Semlar lies off the main road a few miles and is accessed by a jeep trail which has, as the daily motorized traffic, a couple of trucks and a beat-up bus that somehow manage to ford the river. Other traffic includes big-wheeled wooden carts pulled by water buffalo or lordly white oxen, an occasional bicycle with fat tires, and many people on foot. No rain has fallen for weeks, so the dust is ankle deep. I feel as if I am walking in feathers.

I am not sure the villagers have seen many westerners before, because wherever I go, I am followed by a group of curious children. Beside my house is a water buffalo stable, and one gave birth an hour ago to a calf, tiny and pretty, like a fawn. He is already standing spraddle-legged, looking for milk. In the lower floors of the houses in the village, large clay vats hold the fermenting grain that becomes *raksi*, the moonshine of Nepal.

In the evening the men return from the fields with large wooden-wheeled wagons full of grain, and women carry baskets slung back with straps across their foreheads. Others balance urn-shaped water jugs on their heads, walking with perfect posture. And the children come, herding the goats and carrying the smallest in their arms.

▲

I rise to wash before it is light. I walk a quarter mile to the village well. Other women are already there with water jugs. They are used to me now and even take my bucket and fill it out of turn. I say thank you in English since there is not really a word for it in Nepali—only *danybaad*, which is used by foreigners. There is not even a concept for it in Nepali, because you do not expect to be given thanks for doing what is required of you by your *dharma*, religious duties. What you are required to do in this life is all predetermined by what you did in your past life. Your responsibility is to simply perform the tasks well for that will determine in what position you will be reborn. "We do not," a Nepali explained to me, "envy those who have more than we do, for we know that person is simply reaping the rewards of well-performed *dharma*; nor do we feel ashamed of our own lack of things, for we know if we perform our required duties well, in the next reincarnation, we, too, will realize the rewards."

It is much too early for *bhaat*, so I walk to the shallow river just as the sun is coming into view above the trees. The dust ripples gently as I place my feet. A large herd, forty or more, of magnificent white and brindled cattle with large humps float in a golden haze. They mill around quietly and drink from the shining stream. Someone has placed an offering of rice and flowers on a leaf mat in the cleft of the tree by the road.

At nine I walk to the *bhaat* shop where a trainer has arranged my meals for a fixed price. Already hundreds of flies hover. I can see the *didi* stirring a pot in the little kitchen. She scatters the baby goats that are stealing from the flour container. They protest with infant cries. She reaches in for more flour.

When I have finished my *bhaat*, I go to the school for my practice teaching. Classes run from 10 a.m. to 4 p.m., but mine are over by one o'clock. In class, too many children to count crowd together on the benches. I have taught them a litany already.

What is my husband's name? *Mero shrimaanko naam?*

Jim! They shout.

What is my eldest son's name? *Jetho chhorako naam?*

Tim! They shout.

What is my youngest son's name? *Kaanchho chhorako naam?*

Lon! They shout.

How old am I? *Mero umer?*

You are forty-eight years old!

Then we begin counting around the room in English to forty-eight, each child jumping up to shout the number in turn. We only reach half the students so tomorrow I will start on the other side.

The students have memorized the book but have no idea what any of it means. "In," I say, after realizing the day before that their ability to recite this whole lesson had nothing to do with understanding the concept. I take a safety pin and put it in my soap box lid. "The pin is in the box." Then I hand a child a pin. "In," I say. "Put the pin in the box." A delighted grin spreads over his face. He drops the pin in the soap dish.

When my classes are done, I leave and stop at the *chiyaa* shop for tea. The kettle boils on the clay stove fueled by a stick of wood. Already the thermometer attached to my pack reads eighty-six degrees. The village children who have not been in school gather around the table like the ubiquitous flies, settling closely beside me as I begin to write. They recede slightly when I look up.

I try to finish my lesson plans before dark because the electricity routinely fails. The text is an antiquated one in British English. For sixth class a complicated narrative about an English game using terms like "right out" and "left out" comprises the next lesson. I puzzle over the narrative, trying to see any relevance for Nepal. I am straining to understand why learning English is perceived as a priority in a country where one in five children dies before her fifth birthday.

I cannot resist walking west of the village to watch the sunset over the Terai. By the irrigation pond, the birds gather, colorful and foreign. A black and white fisher flies over the pond, followed by a small turquoise bird I do not know. As I move closer to the water to see better, I realize the pond is teeming with snakes. I had thought the circles were fish rising, but now I can see their forms. I turn in surprise to the little girls who are following me. "Snakes," I say, pointing. "See the snakes?" "*Thulo serp*," they reply. Big snake.

When it is time for evening *bhaat*, the stars are out and the electricity as well. I walk down the road in the warm dust with a kerosene lantern. When I return the dust has cooled to velvet. Orion is climbing over the horizon as it did on autumn evenings when I stood as a child in the dust of the farm lane in Iowa. And just for a moment I forget what country I'm in.

"How beautiful are the feet..." the minister said, but he did not mean my grandma's feet. Her big toes twisted abruptly back on the smaller ones and a painful bunion shone a dull red on her right foot. The ugly knob was the result of wearing her older brother's worn-out shoes, she told me. With nine children, only a few could buy new shoes each year. On warm evenings we sat on the steps of the back porch, and Grandma soaked her feet in the grey basin with the white flecks. I would watch her feet, swollen and sore, until the water turned as grey as the basin from the barnyard dust. The cats flopped on their sides and thumped their tails on the crooked sidewalk. The first fireflies began to blink in the cornfield when the sky changed to darker blue.

Woman carrying wood, Semlar

2

When your life is simplified to an elemental level, amazing satisfaction can be gained from doing the most basic tasks well. Yesterday afternoon I walked a short way from the village to the stream where two little girls were doing the family wash. I watched for a while. Although the sun hung low in the sky, I walked back to my room, got my sack of dirty clothes, and returned to the stream. I walked out in the water and mimicked the girls' actions exactly.

First I plunged the shirt up and down in the water that swirled softly around my knees, getting my *lungi*, the tubular piece of material I wear as a skirt, wet. Then I spread the shirt on a smooth warm rock at the bank. I rubbed the soap until I had raised a foamy white lather. I gathered the shirt into a smooth mound and kneaded it like bread dough. Next I spread it out and checked for spots that didn't come clean. I twisted it into a long rope and swung it above my head, slapping it vigorously down on the smooth stones as the little girls did.

It was time for the rinse. I plunged the shirt up and down again and held it in the water where the ripples slid over in little rapids until the soap was gone. I wrung the shirt tightly, set it on the grass, then repeated the process with the green skirt.

As I finished, the sun, a huge red ball, hovered in a dusty haze. I stepped from the water and for one brief instant, my feet were clean. I gathered my clothes and started back. I wanted to stay ahead of the water buffalo that were being driven home. Fourteen black shapes walked on a soft red cloud in front of the sun. I spread my clothes on the roof, for though the nights are cooler now, by mid-morning the sun burns, and they will all be dry.

Washing clothes in Semlar

▲

We liked wash days for we could play in the cellar, riding the scooter around the furnace with the huge arms. We could play in the cob pile with the clean red cobs, but we could not play in the coal bin because of the black dust. My mother would heat the water for the wash in an oblong boiler on the black stove in the kitchen and carry it down the stairs. When the sheet went through the wringer, it would swell in a balloon where the air was trapped. It was like the cow, my brother said, like underneath the cow. "Udder," my mother said, "it's called an udder." We laughed and laughed and laughed.

▲

I have awakened several times to the sound of the rats. I am sweating with fear, but the air is cold. My sleeping bag is on the floor, and I think of the rats crossing my face. I keep the flashlight on. I see the eyes coming around the curve of the big vat that holds the *raksi*, and I shine the light full on them. Each time, when I awake, I am in a vivid homesick dream for a world that has long since ceased to exist.

▲

There were rats in the barn on my grandmother's farm where we lived. Once when I was a child, one slid through the grain chute and landed on my chest. I screamed and screamed. My uncle came from milking the cow, thinking I was hurt.

▲

In the barn in winter it was still very cold, but not as cold as outside where the water would freeze several inches on the cement tank. It would have to be chopped with the ax. In the barn the snow would melt from the horses' backs and steam would rise from the wet hair. It was like the steam from the pail of warm milk where my Uncle Jim leaned his forehead against the small black cow. The milk came in alternating streams and the metallic sound changed as the pail became full.

▲

Once upon a time there was a little girl named Barbara and she lived on a farm in Iowa. And in the winter toward evening the stars would begin coming out while there was still a long line of blue in the west, and sometimes the moon would shine in a thin golden hoop with a heavy-sided rim as the daylight faded. Right at that time was when the little girl and her mother would put on their big coats and their black overshoes with the buckles and their warm mittens.

And do you know what they would do?

> *I know, I know! (Two little blond heads bobbed up and down.)*

What?

> *GET THE MILK! (They shouted in unison.)*

That's RIGHT!

They would walk down to the old milkhouse that sagged against the big barn to get the milk. And because it was winter in Iowa it was very, very cold. And do you know how the snow sounds when it's very, very cold?

> *I know, I know!*

How?

> *(They pantomimed the shuffle with their feet.)*
>
> *Crunch-squeak, crunch-squeak, crunch-squeak!*

That's RIGHT!

And they would walk down through the cold twilight to the milkhouse going crunch-squeak, crunch-squeak, crunch-squeak over the hard snow, and the stars would get brighter and twinkle in the icicles that were hanging from the milkhouse roof like silver arrows. And they would get the milk. Do you know where it was?

> *I know, I know!*

Where?

ON THE HOOK!

That's RIGHT!

The small silver pail was hanging on the hook that was high enough so the cat couldn't reach it to lap any milk out. So Barbara had to stand on her very tippy-toes and her mama held the handle, too, to reach the pail and bring it down carefully. Then the little girl and her mother carried the pail of warm milk that steamed slightly in the cold night air back to the house together.

Lon: Hurry up, Mama, the next part's best.

One evening just when the stars were coming out and the moon was a golden hoop with a heavy-sided rim, do you know what Barbara said?

I know, I know!

Lon: It's my turn, Tim did it last night.

All right, now Timmy, be quiet. Don't say it.

Lon: She said, she said (he stumbled a little because the others always talked so fast and he was afraid they wouldn't wait), she said, I want to do it ALL BY MYSELF!

That's RIGHT!

She said, I want to do it ALL BY MYSELF! Now her mother didn't want her to do it all by herself because mothers are just like that, you know. Besides, it was twelve degrees below zero. It was the COLDEST night of the year. BRRRRRRRRRRRRRR!

Two little boys stood up and shook.

BRRRRRRRRRR!

But her mother let her go because mothers have to sometimes. Barbara put on her big coat and her black overshoes with the buckles and her warm mittens and she walked crunch-squeak, crunch-squeak, crunch-squeak over the snow ALL BY HERSELF past the icicles that were twinkling like silver arrows and into the milkhouse and she reached up to get the pail of milk. And do you know what happened?

   I know, I know!

What?

   IT FELL ON HER HEAD! They screamed.

That's RIGHT!

It fell on her head, and she was so surprised she sat down on the floor. It knocked off her hat and spilled all over her hair and do you know what she did?

   (They were breathless with concern now and Lon's lower lip trembled and Tim had to say it.)

   She cried.

That's RIGHT!

She cried! And her Uncle Jim came out of the barn to see what was the matter and the cat came and tried to lick the milk that was freezing in puddles. And her Uncle Jim picked her up and smiled and held her mitten as they walked over the squeaky snow to the house. The milk froze in icicles like silver arrows in her hair. And her mother was watching from the window and when she opened the door do you know what she said?

   They shouted together happily, the words tumbling,

   SHE SAID, I LOVE YOU, BARBARA!

That's RIGHT!

And I love YOU and now it's time to go to bed.

   Lon: Mama.

What?

   Lon: I know who that little girl is.

I BET you DON'T!

Lon: Un-huh. It's you, Mama.

How did you know, Lonners?

Lon: Because her name is Barbara.

You're so SMART!

Tim: And she lives in Iowa.

That's right, Timothy Tiger.

Tim: Does our dad live in Iowa?

Yes.

Tim: But we live in Oregon.

We live in Oregon.

Tim: But he still loves us, right?

Of course he does, Timmy.

Lon: I want a dad that lives in Oregon.

I know you do, Lonners, but we don't always get what we want.

Lon: Do we get it someday?

Sometimes.

Lon: I want it RIGHT NOW!

What do you want RIGHT NOW?

Lon: You know. A dad that lives in Oregon.

▲

Finally it is morning. I have given up trying to sleep. Already I hear the soft murmur of women passing the house on their way to the well. The water buffalo shuffles in the straw and lows softly to her calf. Tiny goats and children awake with identical cries.

3

This morning I was awakened early by a small boy playing an instrument that sounded for all the world like Tim's violin, but when I looked, it was a hollowed-out piece of wood. It was very roughly carved and the bowl was covered with ragged leather, but the sound was sweet and haunting. I had a mental picture of Tim as a child, standing by the fireplace with his violin tucked under his chin. This boy was crippled and he was going from house to house playing for money. Musicians are a special caste. They are hired for festive occasions, but they lead hard and hungry lives. Nepal's officially outlawed caste designations seem quite pervasive in actual practice. I gave the boy a few rupees, and I have been thinking of Tim all day.

Tim included a self-portrait in his last letter. When I try to explain that my son is an artist, Nepalis look at me in wonder. Except in educated circles in Kathmandu, art here seems still deeply rooted in the religious tradition. Its study as an academic pursuit would be odd and superfluous.

But the children love to draw! I found that out last week when I reviewed the body parts with the fourth class I am teaching in Semlar. I drew a picture of a boy named Ram and a girl named Sita, the Nepali equivalent of Dick and Jane. I had quite a time convincing the children to draw the pictures. First I had them tear a page from their ragged little notebooks. This was obviously a new procedure and everyone had to help each other get it right. Then we got everyone's name on the papers, another community project. I thought I was telling them in perfect Nepali to draw the picture. I had practiced the speech on the trainer. They all lowered their eyes. I tried again. "*Uta,*" stand up, I commanded the "first boy," Ram Chandra. They all have numbers that are based, I'm told, on last year's exams. He stood up. I repeated my speech. He looked around nervously, then he leaned down and began to draw. A collective hum rippled through the room and all the students picked up their pens. Another noisy community project began. After a few minutes I tried to collect the papers. *"Ma laai dinus na."* Give them to me. Again, I had to get Ram Chandra's paper first. Now they want to do a picture every day, and some are quite detailed and good.

Tim is my *jetho chhora*, oldest son. Through him I have established in Nepal my very right to existence as a woman—certainly my right to any exclusive attention from my husband. He is the one on whom the most food and favor would be bestowed. *"Dui janna chhora,"* two sons, I reply, when I am asked how many children I have. The Nepalis beam approvingly. *"Chhori chhaina?"* You have no daughters? *"Chhori chhaina,"* I say sadly, and they smile, for that is not a serious loss, that is merely an inconvenience in a world where women work so hard.

Your father was deliriously happy when you were born, Tim. He went up and down the halls of the hospital saying, "I have a son! I have a son!" and the nurses laughed and told me. And when we brought you home he put on the record and danced with the bundle of you in his arms, singing with the Beatles, "Here comes my son, it's been a long and lonely winter." I was absurdly relieved and felt I had done something that was right.

Boy playing a violin-like instrument

4

Never have I appreciated Lon's struggle to compensate for his dyslexia more than I have in the past few months while I have been learning the Nepali language. It's partly the physical difficulty of having the letters be indecipherable squiggles. The unfamiliar shapes hang by their tops from the line instead of standing firmly on the line below. The most threatening part of the language training at first was the psychological strain of being so slow when twenty-four-year-olds, fresh from college and language courses, deftly fashioned phrases and went off to play while I memorized lists of words. What a battle it is not to feel stupid, even when I have academic credentials to recite to myself in the dark. What did Lon feel as a child with no such comforting assurances of past academic success? I even stutter when called on in class, like he did in the third grade. Was there this gap for him, with the idea, even some of the words, formulated in his mind, but the chasm to expression so deep?

Even as I struggle to gain a minimal competency in Nepali, I am aware that it is only one of almost fifty languages for Nepal. Many villages do not speak it at all, as the first formal schools were not introduced in the rural areas until the 1950s. In Pokhara, where I have just been assigned to a permanent post, several languages are spoken. The family I will live with speaks Gurung. Just east of Pokhara, the villagers speak Tamang.

Yet my assignment is to teach English. English begins in the schools in fourth class, and there is talk of lowering it to first class. I find this amazing. The majority of people in Nepal still don't read or write in any language. An optimistic estimate is that forty percent of the entire population is literate. For women that statistic is between twelve and fifteen percent. The girls in villages are often not sent to school at all, especially after the fifth class when school is no longer free. Somehow Nepalis have been inculcated with the idea that the ticket to change is to speak English. And if it's just change they want, no doubt there's some truth in that.

Except for some improvement in sanitation and general health standards that surely would be best addressed in indigenous languages, I wouldn't want to change much here. Nepal is incredibly rich in natural beauty and inhabited by people who seem unusually adept at having a good time with the simple pleasures of singing and dancing. While no doubt ethnic tensions exist, it is a most tolerant and peaceful society on the whole for all its linguistic variety.

But I admit, I'm grateful I'm having to struggle with just one of their fifty languages, because it's threatening enough to be bad at it. I guess I'll concentrate more on enjoying the dancing with the Nepalis, because that, thankfully, takes no language at all!

Oh, Lon, you are the child who almost wasn't. I knew I had no right to be pregnant and hadn't meant to be. I was so afraid, for I knew by then I would be alone as my mother was alone. I had the paper in my hand, the date assigned, but I ran away. I took a whole bottle of aspirin in Cheyenne, Wyoming. But I wanted too much to live. I put my finger down my throat again and again. And we both lived and you were such a lovely child.

5

How strange a mid-life redefinition of my commitment to my marriage would seem to my Nepali acquaintances. A marriage in Nepal is not something that requires soul-searching and psychological introspection of the partners. The internal questions asked would not be, "Does this marriage meet my needs and expectations, does it allow for my individual growth?" If asked at all, the single question would be, "Can I fulfill the social and religious duties that this role demands of me?"

I had a conversation with Bhumi Paudel, our chief trainer, about marriage tonight. Bhumi is a few years younger than I am, so I can call him Bhumi-*baai*, which means younger brother. This makes all the Nepalis laugh as they call him Bhumi-*daai*, older brother, which conveys respect for both his advanced age and position. I've been able to have some pretty open conversations with him about politics and religion, so I was delighted when he showed up at Semlar today. I have been puzzled by two little girls I saw with red dye in their hair parts, which connotes marriage.

Bhumi was pleased that my Nepali had finally progressed beyond the baby talk stage. For a reward, I think, he chatted with me for a long time in English over evening *daal bhaat*. He said the little girls were probably married, all right, even though the government officially discourages childhood brides these days. His own parents had been married when his mother was eleven and his father seventeen. In a country where medical and economic futures were uncertain, parents felt it expedient to make arrangements for their offspring early. He had been allowed to wait until his twenties because of his studies, even though he was from the Brahmin caste that tended to marry early.

But his marriage was arranged, of course, by his parents. Yes, he had only one wife, he laughed, amused at the delicate way I tried to frame the question. One was quite enough, as he had two daughters and a son. Only when the first wife produced no son to fulfill religious obligations was polygamy officially sanctioned.

He had not known his wife before they were married. That was the custom. She was a Brahmin from a village several hours away. It would not have been socially acceptable then to marry out of caste. Indeed, even when customs are changing, most families still feel strongly about this issue. He was pleased at his father's choice. She was a very good wife, and they had been married more than twenty years. He had found many of the modern ways attractive, but he was still puzzled that western young people wanted to choose their own spouses. Some Nepalis were even emulating that now in Kathmandu. Wasn't it true that in America there was much divorce? And was it true as well that there were many children left without fathers to care for them?

So then it was my turn. There I was in the flickering kerosene light in the *bhaat* shop, trying to explain to Bhumi what marriage is in America. And it was hard. I was reluctant to be open about my own marriage history. Would he have reacted to my divorce with the same judgement I would have given him for two wives? I talked in general terms of emotional and intellectual compatibility. I didn't bring up anything about sex, since that is not politely discussed in Nepal. I did say that many people in America now choose not to marry at all. And some—I didn't mention Jim and me—live together for an extended time before making a formal commitment. He seemed amused at that. "Perhaps they are afraid," he said.

Well, yes, I thought later in the dark. I was. And so was he. But now we've been together seventeen years, and married twelve. It's still there for us, whatever marriage is in America.

In some ways marriage must be easier in Nepal. It is more an economic and social arrangement with clear responsibilities of procreation and getting people fed. Here, husband and wife are more a part of an extended family labyrinth instead of the lonely one-to-one intensity demanded of marriage partners in the U.S.

When it comes to companionship, I'm told, the women stick to women and the men to men.

Not many of us from home would accept the kinds of rigid roles and clearly delineated tasks of marriage in Nepal, even if this would stabilize the fragile institution the legal union has become in our society. Not I, certainly, with the ambivalence I've felt toward the traditional constraints American society still projects on wives and mothers. But it might be worth a try to stop asking whether marriage gives enough to *me* and concentrate a little more on whether I can give enough to *it*.

6

Kathmandu
December

I rode eight hours on the bus from Semlar to Pokhara, a beautiful ride up through the *pahaad*, the rugged foothills of the Himalayas, into central Nepal. I chose to sit on the roof, surrounded by young men and the overflow of commerce including a crate of green parrots and two goats. Early in the evening the bus arrived in the Pokhara valley, which lies at the foot of the Annapurna Massif. The gigantic peaks were still pink with alpenglow when the dusty bus pulled into the station.

I spent a few days getting squared around with my housing and school assignment before I returned to Kathmandu. In Pokhara I met the headsir (principal) of Byndabasini School, who seemed nice and is glad I am coming. My school looks like all the other Nepali schools—small rooms, no electricity, and hundreds of kids. I stammered my way through the introduction and background information. No one at the school speaks much English, which is rather surprising since Pokhara is such a trekking center.

For the outrageous price of thirty-five dollars a month, I will share the upstairs of a brand new home with cold running water and electricity. It belongs to a Gurung family. The father, Bojh Gurung, is a Gurkha soldier with the British in Hong Kong. He's in the Middle East now and drives an ambulance in a British regiment. He had the house built this year with the money he had saved. His wife Chanda, his two small sons Bisal and Biswas, and his mother live downstairs.

Shelby, a young American who will be teaching at the Institute of Forestry, found this place when riding around on her bike, and she invited me to live with her. The windows even have screens. The possibility this offers for sanitation control is positively intoxicating.

An interesting problem surfaced at an educational conference yesterday. Thirty-five "foreign experts" and the headsirs from their assigned schools met to resolve apprehensions. A concern of several of the headsirs was that the foreigners in their villages would not observe proper etiquette in treatment of the lower castes. What was supposed to be a meeting designed to help bridge cultural gaps got off to the wrong start, with some volunteers proselytizing about democracy.

This raises an interesting dilemma. What do you do as a culturally sensitive development worker when elements of the system you are trying to be sensitive to are basically abhorrent to your own values? People who are wonderfully tolerant when it comes to religion seem to have a little more trouble with the caste issue. The women in the group make no bones whatsoever about their intentions to enlighten Nepali women to the possibilities of change from their present subordinate status. It seems easy. We're right and they're wrong.

But what if the Nepalis came over to the U.S. and started telling Iowa beef farmers that it was wrong to kill cows? Or what if the Saudi Arabians came and told women in New York that it was wrong for them to drive cars? Is this what is meant by cultural imperialism? A "culturally sensitive" development worker is beginning to seem a contradiction in terms.

I am relieved to return to my running. I have been going early in the morning before most of Kathmandu is awake. Usually, the first Nepalis I encounter are the women, entering the small *mandirs*, temples, carrying plates of rice and flowers. I think of Jim's mother and her daily faithfulness to Mass.

Religion is such an integral part of daily life here. It is a complex blend of Hinduism, Buddhism, and ethnic customs. Oddly, I am not very curious to understand specifics. The practices seem part of a spirituality common to all cultures. I do not need to know to what manifestation of what god the *pujaa* is being offered to feel that the woman who carries the plate of colored rice and flowers

Woman offering pujaa *at a temple in Kathmandu*

is asking for compassion and love for her family, just as my mother-in-law does each morning in her prayers.

The symbols are far from those I grew up with on the Iowa farm, where cows were killed for livelihood, where that austere little white church at the edge of the cornfield was the only representation of the god. In Nepal, not only are the cows protected, the symbols for god are visible in a plethora of forms. Even the trees are given offerings of flowers. A dizzying array of divinities in various manifestations require homage in colorful celebrations. Such a liberation of the spiritual. Each festival is an Alleluia Chorus set in polychromatic splendor. My favorite personage is the baby Krishna. Stories of his life are told to children to teach them kindness and respect. He's a chubby Christ-child figure, pictured with his mother. The pose is much like the classic western Madonna and Child, but the figures are clothed in colorful eastern dress— and Krishna's skin is blue!

For a long time my feet did not touch the floor when I sat in the straight-backed pew between my mother and my grandmother. My brother sat on the other side of my mother, which made us a family, but we were not a real family. A real family was like Jeanette Wilcox's family who sat in the pew behind us with both a mother and a father. Our father, which art in heaven, only our father had run away.

Sometimes the sun would slant sideways through the window and light up the minister's hair, which meant he was like god.

After the sermon was over the men reached the long-handled pans down the rows. I put in my nickel with a buffalo on it. The buffalo had all gone away, too. My hand smelled funny because it was wet from holding the money.

On special Sundays Uncle Jim and another man passed silver plates with bread cut into small squares. Uncle Jim did not smile at me when he held the plate across me for my mother to take a piece. This is my body, broken.

Then Uncle Jim carried the wooden tray with the little glasses carefully so the blood would not spill. The sun from the minister's head would twinkle in the bottom of the glasses. This is my blood.

We walked to the cemetery carrying the wreaths which smelled like

Christmas. I put the wreath over the flag, for that meant a ▨
died for god.

All the people in the cemetery were dead as my grandpa w▨
they were still Presbyterians. To be a Catholic was bad because they wor-
shipped false images and a man called the pope. But even worse than
the Catholics were the women in the shiny magazines Aunt Bess brought
for my grandma to read. These women were brown and did not cover
their breasts, for they did not know about god.

Kali, the black goddess

IV

THE GOD IN YOU

Didi ra bahina, *big and little sisters*

1

Pokhara
January

A few days ago as I walked past a woman sitting in the sun on a dusty patch of grass, breastfeeding her baby and singing her heart out, I felt a strange wave of emotion. She so obviously was enjoying life that I stopped and smiled. She smiled back and went right on singing. Then I felt a rush go through me that felt dangerously close to resentment. Why are people so happy in Nepal? It's one of the poorest nations in the world and by materialistic western standards, most of the population lives in a state of acute deprivation. Yet they're so laid back about it all. Take last week at school, for example. I knew we had some sort of ceremony for the parents coming on Wednesday, but I didn't know it would wipe out the whole week.

We're scheduled to have school six days a week. That's what the elaborate chart that hangs by the headsir's desk implies. It shows exactly where each teacher is to be all day. A log book lies on a table beneath the chart for teachers to sign in and out. This meticulous attention to schedules and detail perpetuates a myth that must be left over from the colonial influence that drifted up from India, as it has little to do with the way the school really operates.

I went to school Sunday morning. School doesn't start until ten this time of year. I expected to teach my fourth, fifth, and sixth division classes. I did meet my fifth class. It's my most challenging group, with a daily attendance that has fluctuated from fifty-eight to eighty-seven. The room is so crowded that I'm scared I'll find a child smothered like a little chicken at the end of the period. I cope with these conditions by working up the lessons into jazz-rap type chants that alternate words and clapping. Sample (lesson is on indirect objects—we chant in accented beats):

Did I give the pen to her? (clap) dum diddy dum dum, dum, dum, dum.

No, I gave the pen to him. (clap) dum diddy...etc.

But that period was the end of the lessons for the day, as all afternoon was spent with the sixth class practicing a drill routine for the ceremony. This, for reasons unclear to me, resulted in the whole school's shutting down. Monday the same thing happened. By Tuesday I was getting suspicious, and sure enough, there were no classes at all that day. We spent the day, teachers and students together, picking up leaves, sweeping the packed dirt in the court-yard clean with stiff stick brooms, and pasting triangular pieces of paper on string to make the long colored streamers that we stretched across the school yard.

The ceremony itself was on Wednesday. We all came at seven-thirty to pick up the leaves that had blown down during the night and to string up the streamers. We dragged all the benches out of the classrooms and set up a space for the parents and the *thulo maanchhes*, big shots, who were coming. A sound system was rigged up with a car battery for the music and the speeches.

What a lovely day. The headsir introduced all the *thulo maanchhes* and he introduced me, although he only said volunteer instead of identifying me as American. A myriad of organizations volunteer in Nepal and to be from the U.S. does not bring automatic respect, in fact, the opposite right now. Nepal does not view the Gulf War through North American eyes. Daily demonstrations against the war occur in front of the United States Embassy in Kathmandu. A volunteer I know was pushed roughly out of a Muslim shop in Pokhara last week. Mohammad, one of the bright-est boys in sixth class, has stopped coming to English. After my headsir introduced me, I gave a little speech in my woefully in-adequate Nepali. The teachers and parents all smiled approvingly, because at least I had tried.

All Nepali ceremonies include dances, and the boys and girls who danced were graceful and beautiful. By now, even I know the familiar stories of the dances. We all laughed uproariously, and the littlest children watching were so excited that a long bench tipped and spilled them all onto the ground.

The students who had done well on their last year's exams were given copies of the new year's textbooks wrapped in brightly colored paper, and red *tika*, rice paste, was put on their foreheads and shoulders. Then a funny thing happened. When the *thulo maanchhes* began to give their speeches, the sound system completely failed and could not be coaxed back to life. So the *thulo maanchhes* stood close to each other and gave their speeches anyway, while people in the audience talked quietly with each other and the little children squirmed and drew pictures in the dust.

I had been taking photos, but someone brought a chair for me. When I sat down, a little girl from the fourth class moved over to my lap, followed by her little sister, who had to be taken up as well. The sun was warm on my back and the large black kites circled above the terraced fields behind the school, looking for prey.

The dancing went on and on, and finally I wandered off and started home. I was not at all surprised that the headsir had announced a holiday for Thursday to celebrate the successful ceremony. I found I really didn't mind at all, because that meant I could take my binoculars and hike up the trail that leads behind the Buddhist monastery through the rows of tattered prayer flags fluttering in the wind. Just last week I saw a serpent eagle perched in a snag up there.

Suddenly I understood the strange feeling I experienced when I saw the singing woman on the grass. It was not resentment at all; it was envy. Envy for the people in a little, poor country that does not seek wars; envy for people who take all the time they need to enjoy life.

*The morning exercise routine at
Byndabasini School*

2

I was told soon after I came to Byndabasini that Hari had once killed a man. Hari is almost a foot taller than the other Nepali men at my school. He served as a Gurkha soldier with the British army for ten years and after that he was with the Indian army for another decade. But he did not kill the man in war. It was an accident during a soccer game, when he kicked the ball so hard that it snapped the neck of the man it hit. This is what I was told by Indu Parajuli, another teacher, when we were standing in line for the exercises, a morning ritual that serves as physical education for the school.

"Double up, double up!" Hari bellows to the students who are straggling through the gate, little sisters and brothers in tow, flip-flops slapping their heels as they scurry to their places in the long lines. Does he mean to say "hurry up" or is "double up" a military term? I never ask, because I wouldn't want to be suggesting a misuse of English. Then the drum begins. Thump, thump, thump, thump... Thump-a-thump. And the students, approximately one thousand of them, straighten to attention. Sort of.

First class is still giggling and pushing. One of the teachers rounds up the tenth class boys who are leaning with practiced indolence against the railing by the upper school classrooms. They slouch lazily to their places in line while Hari glares at them. A few students are exempt from this exercise routine because it is their turn to clean the classrooms. They stir dust that rises from the open doorways in large brown balloons over the lines closest to the building. Then the drum begins again.

Thump, thump, thump, thump.

Thump, thump, thump, thump.

The routine of exercises, which looks to me like a videotape of soft aerobics for a geriatric ward, begins. Four reaches to the left, four to the right, half turns and march in place. It is long, complicated, and practiced. At the end, when the drum beats have become conspicuously louder for several measures, ending with thump-a-thump, they all, even the teachers, stand at attention and sing the national anthem. It is a quavering little melody that ripples through the students. At the end they all salute the place where the flag will stand when we get one some day, and they say "Nepal."

Then the harangue begins. Hari selects a row. Today it is the eighth class girls. I don't have to know all the vocabulary to understand. He scolds them for their lackadaisical participation in the exercises. He mimics their dainty, languid movements. They giggle. Then he turns to the sixth class boys. They have not sung forcefully enough, he says, and he imitates their fragile tone. They laugh. He seems a friendly giant.

But when he turns to the tenth class boys, he is really scolding. This is for Nepal. They are lazy. *"Alchhi,"* he repeats several times. Lazy, lazy, lazy. They must come on time. They must be a good example for the younger students if Nepal is to be strong. The boys do not laugh. They merely stare in the distance as teenagers do everywhere.

Then the drum begins again at a more rapid tempo. Thump-thump-thump and row by row they march toward their classrooms for roll-taking. Boys dump yesterday's garbage over the fence behind the school. Girls sweep the steps and the porch with small stick brooms.

I wait for Hari. We do not talk much. He is ashamed of his English after ten years with the British. I understand. *"Ma laai Nepaali gaarho laagyo."* I find Nepali difficult, I always tell him. But we have a daily routine.

"Americamaa?" In America? He means do we do exercises like these in America.

"Yes." I lie, for that is what they think and that is what he expects to hear. I could never explain the part of the school budget that goes to athletics in America.

"Naraamro bidyaarthi!" Bad students, he shakes his head.

"Mero bichaarma, raamro bidyaarthi!" In my opinion, good students. This is what he wants me to say, but I mean it, too.

"No discipline!" he complains.

"Americamaa, ustai." In America, the same, I commiserate. And there we usually part, but today there is more. He has heard the news.

"America very strong," he says. "Smart bombs! So many bombs! One bomb, *kati parchha?"* How much does one bomb cost?

"Tahaa chhaina." I don't know. I hate these questions.

"America very, very rich. Many, many bombs."

"Dheari." Many. I can't dispute that.

"Nepalmaa, no discipline," he grumbles again. "Many years we will be like America. Smart bombs."

"No, Hari." In America I would put my hand on his arm to emphasize the point, but women do not touch men in Nepal. "Not smart bombs. Smart students."

He looks amused. I'm not sure he understands what I mean. But he likes the phrase he has heard on the news. "Smart bombs," I hear him say to himself as we part.

Sherpa boy with his meal, Lukla

3

When Lon was a child he had a collection of bottle caps. He kept it in one of the drawers of the blue dresser, and for years the bottle caps spilled out on the floor. I, of course, would have loved to have thrown it away because I was always stepping on one of those serrated edges with my bare feet, but it seemed to be an important part of his life at the time, so I left it alone. Finally he hauled the whole thing down to the garbage can and threw it unceremoniously away himself. That whole scene came back with a rush today.

I had gone for tea with the women teachers at my school, as I do every day about one o'clock between morning and afternoon classes. The *chiyaa* shop, like all *chiyaa* shops in Nepal, is a combination business and family living quarters. The place where we sit to drink the tea and have *pau roti*, a western type of bread, is actually the family bedroom. The benches we sit on are slept on at night. Often, there are little kids crawling around them. Sometimes chickens wander in from the backyard.

Today a little boy about three years old came in and crawled under one of the beds. He produced a can that was brimming full with bottle caps. Totally oblivious to our company, he proceeded to string them in elaborate designs all around what little floor space there was. Then, very pleased with himself, he trotted off into the backyard with the chickens.

His unsuspecting mother, meanwhile, harried with an overflow of customers, came back into the room carrying her incredibly crusty black tea kettle and strainer to give us another cup of tea. She wasn't looking down and couldn't have seen the bottle caps anyway, as it was dark and smoky in there and she was facing the

doorway that was glaring with bright midday sun. She hit the serrated edges of those bottle caps with her bare feet and buckled
into a dance that almost showered everybody with the milky sweet
tea. When she got the kettle solidly on the table, she scooped all
the bottle caps into the can the child had abandoned. She did not
throw them away. She set the can back under the bed. We all
had a good laugh, and in my broken Nepali I told my friends about
my *kaanchho chhora*, youngest son, and his bottle cap collection
and they laughed and laughed. We decided that kids all over the
world are probably lugging around their cans of bottle caps.

▲

*January 16th was your birthday, Lon, the very day the Gulf War
started. All day I thought of you. And all night the dogs of Pokhara
barked. I hear them every night now as I hear the old woman in the
shack north of the house. She coughs and coughs. You would be worried. You always worried about such things—stray animals and people
you thought I could help.*

▲

Lon: Mom...

What?

Lon: What happened to the donkey?

*I don't know. They had lots of donkeys then and in some places of
the world they still do, even in the Middle East. There's more to
the story and when you get bigger you can read it. Some people I
know consider it the basis of their religion and the most important story in the world. Maybe you will too. There's another place
in the story where Jesus is riding on a donkey. But after that the
story is very, very sad because Jesus is killed by Roman soldiers.*

Lon: Were the soldiers bad men?

*No, they weren't really bad men, Lon. They were probably pretty
ordinary young boys who were trained to kill. That's what happens in armies. They were just carrying out their government's
orders and like most people, they were pretty loyal to their government.*

Lon: But they were bad if they killed somebody.

I tend to agree.

But from their standpoint, Jesus was a trouble maker. Jesus belonged to a group known as the Hebrews who were giving the Roman government lots of trouble. And governments usually want everybody to follow the rules without asking questions. The Romans had a pretty good government as governments go. They kept peace in the area a long time and built an impressive empire on the resources of people they conquered. But to keep it together they killed lots of people, and Jesus was one of them.

4

One of the children I saw dancing in the street at sunset last week is dead. On Sunday morning he fell into the irrigation canal that rushes like a mill race south of our house. I've taken personal comfort in that rushing sound. It reminds me of Still Creek, which flows past our family cabin on Mt. Hood. Now that the weather is warmer, I often leave the back door open so I can close my eyes and pretend I'm there. But the canal is dangerous, and in an unusual precaution, in a land where the financial cost of safety makes it a luxury, much of the canal has wire over the top. For several feet beside the little bridge on our road the wire is pushed back because the people in the cluster of little clay houses across the street have no other water source. Someone is always dipping water or bathing there. I've thought of the risk to children, but it's easy to become less attuned to that here because life itself is such a dangerous proposition. Daily existence includes a proximity to hazards like fire, animals, and traffic from which our very lifestyle in developed countries shields children.

I had just come back from running. The morning was especially beautiful, with the mountains glowing. I had started up the stairs when there was a commotion and wailing by the canal, and the sound of many people running in sandaled feet. From the shrill, keening cry it was obvious what had happened, and though many people ran as fast as they could along the canal, there was no hope of saving the child. It took over fifteen minutes for the water supply to be cut and the canal to drop and slow to a trickle.

It's distressing how tempting it is to minimize tragedy in another culture by seeking refuge in that most egregious of ethnocentric comments—that they don't value individual life as we do.

I've heard that a lot lately, from westerners about Nepalis, and on the radio from high sources in the American government about the Iraqis.

By the time I left for school they still had not brought the body back. People gathered in clusters by the canal, retelling the story and pointing. Another child, a younger brother perhaps, stood at the spot where the boy had fallen in, weeping inconsolably.

5

The kerosene jug was suspiciously light, so I emptied the remaining liquid into the green Chinese wick stove and set off to replenish our supply. Kerosene was being rationed because of the war in the Gulf, and I hadn't quite mastered the coupon system. Last time I needed some, I found a shopkeeper who felt sorry for me and sold me some of his own hoard. That was worth a second try.

I passed the pond by the rice mill. A lumbering truck from India was brought to a throbbing, honking halt by a parade of unruffled brown ducks that were crossing the road to the water. Then I saw Bonnie. She was walking her bike, so I knew something was wrong.

Bonnie usually manuevered her bicycle with confident aplomb through the array of living species and commerce vehicles that compete for space on the narrow Mahendra Pul road. I often saw her on my way to school, since her house was not far from ours. Westerners are always conspicuous, even when they dress Nepali as Bonnie does. She wears the colorful *punjabis*, the loose pants and tunics that the most progressive young Nepali women wear.

She was not exuding confidence now. Her face was red and her lips were pressed together. She stared stonily ahead as she wheeled the bike through the assorted clutter of the Nepali roadside, not even noticing me until I was right beside her. I grabbed her arm.

"Bonnie, are you all right?"

She jumped back from the contact, almost tipping the bike. Then she recognized me. Her face wrinkled.

"Are you all right?" I repeated. I could tell she was trying not to cry. I turned to walk with her, back toward my house.

"I hate these people," she said, in a high, unnatural voice. "I hate them. I hate them."

"Come have some tea," I suggested. She didn't speak again until we had gone upstairs and I'd started the tea water on the green stove. I tried not to let myself calculate the remaining kerosene.

She'd hit a child. She'd been riding from Mahendra Pul when a little boy had dashed across the street. I pictured it—the quick darting form weaving through the traffic. My hand always unconsciously clapped to my mouth in fear when I saw this on the way to school. Usually, just when I thought the child would certainly be killed, he or she darted behind a cow, and the grey cab would swerve in a practiced arc to miss them both. Dogs often weren't so lucky. Many times I'd heard the sickening thud of a solid hit. A lot of dogs along that street were dragging useless legs.

This time Bonnie hadn't missed. The boy had been knocked down. Luckily, he wasn't killed by the traffic coming the other way. He wasn't even badly hurt. But, of course, a crowd had gathered, and the child had cried and cried.

"I didn't feel a thing," Bonnie said. "You'd think I would have, but all I could think was how stupid they are not to watch their kids."

"Just shock," I observed.

"No," she insisted. For some reason she felt it necessary to make a point. "I didn't feel a thing, I really didn't. I would have felt worse if I hit a dog. They ARE stupid. No wonder this country is so backward."

She was in shock, of course. I'm sure it had been terrible. The sudden impact, the tangle of limbs and wheels, and the gravel rising up to meet them. And then everyone staring and talking so fast. It was a hard time to be an American here anyway. I'd wished for more anonymity today myself as the college students who were discussing the war slowed down to wait for me on the way home from school. "Where are you from? Are you an American? You're an American. Your country is very weak to use its power in such a way." I had kept my eyes down and walked on.

I didn't know what to say to Bonnie. I'd never let my own kids talk the way she just had—or students in my classes at home. But

Bonnie wasn't a kid and it wasn't an opportune time to lecture on the situation in Nepal that led to children in the streets. She knew the facts as well as I.

"Do you want a peanut butter sandwich?" I asked. She did. She followed me back into the kitchen. She wanted to keep talking about the accident, but I was feeling compromised and tried to change the subject.

We talked for a while of neutral things. I knew by tomorrow she'd be embarrassed about what she'd said, and she'd be sure to cultivate a different kind of conversation with me. But I was glad when she finally left.

It was too late to go for kerosene. I didn't want to be without hot water for morning, so I took my cold tea up to the roof to watch the blue evening settle over the Pokhara valley. I was sorry this happened today. I liked Bonnie, really. I especially liked her name, which was one I had picked out for the daughter I never had. This story is only one side of her. She was in Nepal for the same reasons as the rest of us—some vague feeling of wanting to share the abundance our society had amassed.

It's such a jolt to recognize your own naiveté as you try to accept another culture on its terms. How easily we regress to the old ways of thinking about us and them to try to validate ourselves. I wish I could say I'd never had any ethnocentric reactions flash through my mind since I came to Nepal, but it'd be a lie. I didn't like what Bonnie said today, and I'm feeling a little cowardly for not confronting her more directly about it. But I'm painfully aware of my own complicit guilt. I'm part of a generation whose vision of setting the world aright involved making all cultures fit the western mold.

No, I like Bonnie. Most of the time, with her witty one-line quips and easy humor, she seems a nice connection with home. But today she was a connection with a part of home I didn't want to be reminded of right now—how easily, in the heat of emotion, we can lose sight of the humanity of others whose lives are slightly different from our own.

6

At 11:30, when I have finished class 6b, both Indu and I have a free period. Our arrangement is to meet in front of the shrine to the goddess of knowledge. We sit on bamboo mats to review the news we heard on the radio that morning. Indu practices his English and I practice my Nepali. We help each other.

"*Ghaam laageko chha,*" I say. The sun is shining. I always try to get in some small-talk phrases I don't have to think about so it will seem as if I've spoken more Nepali. I'm ashamed to still be so inept at conversing in this language.

"*JaaDo!*" Indu answers and shivers. Then he translates, as he is supposed to be speaking English. "It's cold." I laugh. It seems most pleasant to me sitting there in the sunshine. I am amused at the men who wear scarves around their throats. In the early morning they even wrap them around their faces against what seems to me merely a welcome crispness in the air.

"*Aaja bihana jaaDo thiena.*" This morning it wasn't cold, I insist. Indu shivers again.

"Did you listen to the news?" he asks.

"*My laai BBC sunchhu.*" I listen to BBC.

"*Sunne,*" he corrects. Past tense.

"*My laai BBC sunne.*" I listened to BBC, I repeat.

"I listened to Nepali news and BBC," he asserts. I nod approvingly. "About the war."

"*Laadai kobarremaa,*" about the war, I echo.

"It was very bad," he says slowly. I am dreading this. I was awake all night. I heard the BBC correspondent, Alan Little, with shocked tears in his voice. He was reporting from Baghdad as they brought the bodies from the wreckage of a neighborhood air raid shelter where an American missile went down a heat vent and killed hundreds of civilians.

"*Naraamro samachaar.*" It was bad news, I repeat after him.

"A bomb entered the shelter. There were women and children." He does not look at me. "Women and children," he repeats haltingly, "curled." He stops. "*Ke* curled?" What's curled? "The man said 'curled in sleep.'"

I hold my voice steady. I am teaching, not discussing politics. "Curled," I say after him, trying to think of a Nepali word.

"*Aaimee ra ketaa-keti,*" women and children, "*uniharu le suthie,*" they were sleeping—I am not sure that verb tense is right, but he does not correct me. He is studying me curiously. "Curled." I tuck my head to my chest and bring my knees up. "*Bachaa ustai.*" Like babies. Our eyes lock and there is a long silence. I am the first to look away. He has seen my tears.

Sherpa children standing in front of mani *stones,*
upon which mantras, *prayers,* *are inscribed*

7

The Gulf War has forced me to the brink of a personal crisis that I am only beginning to understand. I have listened incessantly to BBC's accounts—the rain of death on the cities; the experimentation with "Big Blue," a napalm kind of bomb; and the oil in the Gulf. I've heard the speeches, from Bush asking god to bless America at the Superbowl to the king of Jordan claiming that the Allies were launching a savage attack the like of which the world had never seen. I have listened to an international gathering of church leaders in Australia debate the "just-war" concept and I have heard the calls from Iraq for all Muslim nations to join in a holy war.

I'm glad I'm in Nepal. I'd rather deal with the questions and disapproval here than the spectator-sport mentality at home. Protests against the war occur daily in Kathmandu, and some of us have been subjected to verbal taunts here in Pokhara. Both major parties in the upcoming election issued statements urging an end to the hostilities in the Middle East. Only two percent of the people in Nepal are Muslim, however, so there isn't the religious outrage that has surfaced elsewhere. On the whole, it's been calm compared to India or Pakistan.

Nepalis are worried because kerosene is scarce and expensive. Their own political situation is more immediate to them than the war of a rich giant on whom they perceive themselves to be somewhat dependent for economic and technological aid. For the most part, even though I've been uncomfortable about the war, direct conversation is framed politely to me. Even my teacher friends, who know I oppose the war, are careful. "Do you think it could be that Mr. Bush is crazy?" one asked. But the day the ground offensive against the retreating Iraqis began was another story.

That day I stopped on the way home from school at a shop for tea. A man stood up when I walked in. He screamed at me in English. "You are animals; Americans are animals!" He continued screaming, in Nepali by this time, and the tears on my face dried as I felt something within me snap.

When I was in high school we were taken in the big yellow buses to hear Eisenhower at a cornhuskers' rally. The flag was waving. The sky was blue and there was the President of the United States of America, flanked by a young senator from Massachusetts. Behind them was a field of tasseled corn that stretched for miles, dipping in the wind like prairie grass before the white men came. We cheered and cheered. I remember the sun on Eisenhower's head as he bent over the paper he was reading into the microphone. My heart was so filled with pride I could feel a tingling down the inside of my arms. That was nearly half a century ago and half a world away. I'd heard of Nepal only because my grandma read aloud the National Geographic *article about Hillary's first ascent of Everest.*

"Why am I crying?" I thought. It was as if I could physically feel all the magnetic filings within me realigning and focusing toward a different core. "I have done with national loyalties. A country is a place to live. There is a world to love."

I left the shop. The scene had shifted focus for me somehow. It was as if for the first time I really understood that the lives of every one of these Nepali children were as valuable in every way as my own.

I continued walking toward home. On Ram Krishna Tole, I passed the orange house where I often see a green parrot sunning itself on the porch in the morning. A small boy sat there, his feet dangling.

"Hello, mister, one rupee," he said, from habit, not from hope. I stopped and smiled.

"*Maagne naraamro chha.*" Begging is not good. "*Namaste bana!*" Speak the polite greeting. He smiled back and raised his hands.

"*Namaste.*" I salute the god in you.

"Thank you," I said. It is not customary to salute children in return, but I continued, speaking in English. "I salute the god in you, too."

V

IN THE GAZE OF THE SACRED MOUNTAIN

*Machhapuchhare, along
Barbara's running route*

1

Pokhara
February

I ran early yesterday, even though it was Saturday, because any decent speed has to happen before the water buffalo traffic hits the road. The mountains were just ghostly outlines, but the Nepalis were beginning to stir, because they, like me, are clocked by the sun.

I jogged up to the corner that turns left toward the Kathmandu road, then really stretched out at a good clip for about a quarter of a mile. Right before I reached the junction with the main road, two little boys joined me. That has happened before, but they've always dropped back after a few hundred yards. These kept with me so I smiled and told them they were good runners. They stayed right beside me even though I was going fairly fast. They were probably about ten or eleven years old.

We loped along and started the circle back. I could see all the Annapurnas and Machhapuchhare, and they were positively scarlet in the sunrise. We didn't talk much because the boys were breathing a little heavily. We stayed three abreast, I with my $100 Nike AirStabs and they with their little flip-flops, as thong sandals are called here.

"*Thaki laagyo?*" Aren't you tired? I asked.

"No," they lied in English, and we all smiled again and kept running.

The vegetable carts were beginning to appear on the road, and the shopkeepers were out sweeping the dirt in front of their little shops. On previous mornings they had simply stared in silence at the crazy foreigner. Yesterday, with the children running beside me, people broke into delighted smiles and gestured to each other. I waved and smiled, and they smiled back. Then we passed the little mosque. A man stepped through the gate, coming from early morning prayers. He looked a little startled. Then he laughed aloud and clapped. "Bravo!" he called in English. *"Ekdam raamro!"* Excellent.

The boys grinned, even though the littlest one, who had never taken off his jacket, panted, *"Taadhaa?"* Is it far?

"Naajik," near, I said, and slowed to walk down the lane that cuts from the road to my house. I had tears in my eyes that I didn't want them to see, for this year has been a lonelier business than I ever could have imagined.

"Pheri annus," come again, I said. "Keep running and you'll win the Olympics." They regarded me seriously.

"Goodbye," they said politely in English. One raised his hand in a clenched fist salute.

"For Nepal! The Olympics!"

2

I experienced one of those rare, clear images tonight, when a phrase that had been mostly academic and intellectual in my mind became vividly alive, embodied in a particular individual. The phrase was Kipling's "white man's burden."

I had been invited to a dinner at the home of an American nurse. Among the other guests was an Englishwoman, who is what my grandmother, who had no truck with women who chose to live their lives without men, would have called an old maid and a missionary one at that. She was extremely proper and British, and used quaint phrases like "leaving a penny" to describe a Nepali woman's discreet squatting in the street. She's a matron now at the nurses' residence. She came to Pokhara as a nurse herself in 1967. The original missionary medical team that had walked in from northern India in 1952, when the border was first opened to westerners, was still here. That western medical team with the *thulo*, big, doctor Lydia O'Hanlon and the *kaanchhi*, small, doctor Ruth Watson is legendary among development workers in Nepal.

For the most part, contributors from industrialized nations pride themselves on the medical enlightenment they have brought to Nepal. Only in the last few years have westerners given any credence to indigenous medical and healing practices, or has any recognition been extended to the complicated system of food classification and herbal remedies with which the Nepalis had addressed health prior to the coming of industrialized nations. The plethora of western medicines, many of them out of date, sold unrestricted from little kiosks on the streets, attests to the faith of the Nepalis that the knowledge of foreigners will make them well.

I found the woman I met at dinner tonight interesting, charming, and well intentioned. I have tried to copy the phrasing of information and the expressions she used, which conveyed the ambiguous mixture of fondness and condescension she felt for the Nepalis.

▲

It was the providence of God that there was a revolution against the Rana kings in 1952, and the Christians were finally allowed to come in. It's their religion that keeps them down, you know, with all that caste business and how the higher caste won't even use a toilet that a lower caste has used. It's not just the Brahmins, either.

The first medical station was set up not more than a few hundred yards from where we are now sitting. It was an open field then, and there Dr. O'Hanlon performed the first western surgery, which was to take off a man's leg. It was right there in the field out in the open air under the sight of God. Now the kaanchhi *doctor, Ruth Watson, why she had not so much as delivered a baby before she came to Nepal. All she had done was deliver a calf on her brother's farm. Learned her surgery right on the spot, she did, and my, what she could do with a harelip or a bad burn.*

Some land was donated west of town by the Brahmins, and it was there the first permanent structures were set up. "Chunkilo," the Nepalis called it. That meant shining. For they were the metal huts, you know, with the rounded tops, and the sun hit them, so it was the Shining Hospital. There were only forty-four beds, so of course they had to use the floor and outside, too. They took Nepalis who could neither read nor write and trained them in basic nursing to help.

It was in '67 that I came, ten years after Green Pastures, the leprosy hospital, had been established. Leprosy was such a problem. All those people with no noses. There was still no road. I came to be a nursing sister at the Shining Hospital. Now I wasn't a trained doctor, but I learned to be both a doctor and dentist there. I mean, the people were there, so you just had to take care of them, now didn't you? Why I couldn't begin to tell you the number of teeth I've taken out or the fractured arms I've set. And oh, those breast abscesses! So ugly they were, and the smell would like to knock you over. They're so dirty, you know, and the nursing mothers would get infected.

There was a little generator in the operating theatre, but it didn't always work, so many an operation was done by torchlight. In hot weather someone always had to stand by the table with a fly swatter to try to keep the flies from landing. Why, we made our IV fluids in our own still, we did. And then there were the dressings. Baked them in the oven, that's what we did, in newspapers. And I won't tell you how many times we reused them, boiled them in big pots.

I was mostly in the outpatients' building and some days we saw over three hundred patients. People would walk five or six days to come. The clinic would start at 7:30 in the morning and we'd try to close by ten at night. In 1967 there were two doctors, four nurses, and a small team of trained Nepalis. In the hot season when the vomiting and diarrhea was the worst, there'd be so many we'd put them outside. Why, there'd be drip bottles hanging from the trees. And in the cold season it'd be burns upon burns. They sleep too close to the fire, you know. And of course the snake bites or the bear mauls. Now they don't need to die of snake bites, of course, but they will go to the witch doctor first, so by the time we get them, there's nothing for it but to amputate.

And so many babies. Such awful complications. The women would be in terrible condition by the time we got them. They don't come, even now, you know, just squat by the bed and have it, unless there's already something wrong. There's still a high death rate from tetanus. They cut the cord with an unsterile knife. Still, it's a wonder even more don't die. They're considered unclean, the women are, for eleven days after the baby is born. Why, they can't even come back in the house. No wonder they get sick. And some so very young.

It's better now. There used to be so many little girls, twelve, thirteen. That was bad in other ways, too. Sometimes the little things would be married to much older men. Why, the old man would die, but the girl could never marry again. If they got pregnant by another man, God help them. They were thrown out of the village and became casteless. It still happens, you know. Sometimes they can make their way to their own mother's village and be taken back in, but like as not they die.

The worst case I had, though, was a woman from a village whose husband was in India. Not a Gurkha. They're the ones you hear about, because they come back with money, but there's plenty more that go, you know, because there's no work here. They go to India as night watchmen or try to get on anywhere. A lot never come back, you see, probably don't make the money or they die. But the women here are stuck. Well, this woman became pregnant by another man, and there she was with a husband in India. Now they couldn't let anyone know, so the girl and the mother-in-law came down out of the village. They surely didn't intend to come to us, but the girl, she was bleeding like a stuck pig, she was, and they must have thought she was going to die.

We got her stopped all right, but then that night she had the baby. I remember, it was Christmas Eve, it was, I'll never forget it. In the morning I could tell she'd had the baby. Where is it, I said, where's the baby, but they wouldn't tell. And the girl just cried and cried. I grabbed the mother-in-law, I did, and shook her. That little knife they have fell out. Where's the baby, I said again, but she wouldn't tell. Why, she'd thrown it in the rubbish bin, she had. And in I jumped, right in with the rats, I did, and got the baby out. But when I came back in the ward, both girl and mother-in-law went hysterical. Such a screeching it was! The little boy was still alive. But luckily, he died by the next morning, poor little thing. Born on Christmas Eve, he was, but no one in the village would ever know.

We have to obey the regulations, you know. Can't say anything about the church. It's against the law. All you can do is live it. If they catch you teaching it, you have to leave.

I look around and think to myself, what have we done, really? There's so many of them now. Why, Pokhara was a village, and look at it today. Typhoid's less, I will say that. Leprosy's still here, though. Dark skin, you know. Doesn't that make you wonder, just a little? We don't see nearly the big epidemics now, what with the vaccination clinics and all, but there's scarcely a family without TB, and worst of all is plain old malnutrition.

Twenty-four years it's been, almost twenty-five. I have to say, though, England's still home. Why, I've always stayed on three meals a day, I have, and meat, too. I still get homesick. Two more years, maybe, I'll stay, and then I'll go back home for good. I live in York, you know. My little church lies right there in the shadow of the Minster, to the left it is. You know the poet, "Oh, to be in England, now that April's there." Well, it gets me every spring, it does, and someday I'll be there.

Children at Bydnabasini School

3

I've really been enjoying the children here. Since I've always taught high school students at home, this veritable sea of smaller faces staring up at me was a bit intimidating at first. I had to figure out how to deal with the dynamics, but kids are, after all, kids, and I've found that my sons trained me pretty well for what I need to know with this bunch, too.

Take my fourth class, for instance. I have them in the afternoon. I have no idea how many are really in the class, since roll is taken in the morning in a long, complicated procedure that seems to take most of first period and involves each child knowing his or her school number. My daily head count ranges from sixty-five to seventy-five. All the girls sit on one side and all the boys sit on the other. I would like to even out the seating as fewer girls are in the class, but I know better than to suggest such a thing. The degree of discomfort is probably irrelevant anyway.

This class was taught the textbook last year and can recite it by memory. That, I've found, has nothing to do with being able to speak English or having any idea what the phrases they shout mean. The challenge is to rearrange the stilted sentences from their books into dialogue that they might actually use someday.

Classroom management takes on a whole new meaning here. I refuse to carry a stick, which some of the Nepali teachers do. But that has its price, because the kids aren't sure that you mean business without one. So I have to keep the lesson moving quickly.

We start the class with a warm-up exercise. *Uta!* I command, and they all jump to their feet. Except Rishi Ram. He is very, very small and probably enjoys the distinction of being the most squished in class four. Now that he knows I am not going to hit anyone, he has identified this as a way of getting a little attention in a classroom where a teacher by necessity must think group instead of individual. Luckily, he is only three rows from the front of the room. I walk to the end of his row, and each pair of brown eyes follows me. Excuse me, young man, will you please rise? I ask very formally in English he doesn't understand. He shyly stands, eyes averted, trying not to smile.

Touch your eyes! Point to the window! Touch your nose! Pick up a pen! Point to the ceiling! Point to the teacher!

I do NOT say touch the teacher. They loved it the time I did, but they all fell over like dominoes leaning toward me.

Touch your elbow! ELBOW! (That's a hard one.) Touch your toes! (No room for that, everyone squirms downward.)

Point to a girl!

I do NOT say touch a girl, because the boys could never do that.

Basa!

When they have sat down, I quickly command a row on each side of the room to rise. I've found that having only one student stand at a time doesn't demand enough attention. This way they know I will fire my questions at any one of the ones who are standing. Anyone else who does not keep his or her eyes on me is also fair game. *Timiharu,* I say to the row of girls, which means they are all supposed to answer.

Hello, I say in a normal voice.

HELLO! They shout at the top of their lungs, forgetting they are supposed to speak in normal voices to me.

I put my hands over my ears and they all laugh.

Hello, I start again.

HELLO! They shout a little less vociferously.

My name is Barbara. What is your name?

My name is ....(and they all shout their names, because THAT is too exciting to say quietly.)

I live in America. Where do you live?

I live in NEPAL!

Here I have to swing to the other row or I will lose them.

Eklai, alone, *timi,* you, I say, pointing to a boy.

How old are you?

I am.... (there is a consultation with a neighbor)...ten years old.

I point to another.

Timi. How many brothers do you have?

I have four brothers.

I ask the same child, because this always fascinates me.

How many sisters do you have?

I have five sisters.

I continue switching gears from row to row, individual to groups, until we have exhausted the familiar litany I have established. Then I unroll the brown mail packet paper I have prepared to present new material I will begin to use tomorrow. I have drawn a picture of dubious artistic merit of a boy with a dog. The boy wears a white shirt and blue pants, as any normal Nepali school boy would. The dog is black and white. Under the picture are the words in fairly large print.

This is Ram.

Ram is a boy.

His shirt is white.

This is Ram's dog.

Ram's dog is black and white.

Leka! I say, which means write. So they all get out their little notebooks, which are called *kopies*. This is a very serious business for they know they are to draw a picture like mine first. I prowl the skinny aisle between the girls' side and the boys' side, inevitably tripping on someone as I strain to check their progress. Shoba's picture is very small.

Thulo maanchhe, big man, I say, stretching my hands far apart.

Pheri leka! Write again, I say to Krishna, who has started his letters by attaching them to the top line like Nepali letters instead of placing them on the bottom line.

Then I tell them to take the papers home and very carefully copy them neatly to give to me tomorrow. And that means I must move quickly or the ones who are done will start messing around. Since they have been very good today, I clap my hands and when they are all still, I look right at Laxmi who is waiting breathlessly to see whether I will do her favorite one, and say,

Das saano baadarharu (in four even beats)
TEN LITTLE MONKEYS! Sixty-five voices scream.
Bistramaa oo-free-ra-hay-chun.
JUMPING ON THE BED!
Eutaa baadar laudau
ONE FELL OFF!
Ra takomaa katyo!
AND BUMPED HIS HEAD!
U doctor kahaa guy-o
HE WENT TO THE DOCTOR!
Ra doctor lay banyo,
AND THE DOCTOR SAID,
Timi bistramaa na-oof-ra!
YOU STOP JUMPING
ON THE BED!

Again. I raise my hands into snapping position and sixty pairs of hands come up. I begin with ten again to reinforce the sequence.

Ten little monkeys (I start down the aisle snapping my fingers.)
TEN LITTLE MONKEYS! (Snap, snap, snap, snap)
Jumping on the bed! (I skip-hop four times during the line.)
JUMPING ON THE BED! (One hundred and thirty feet bounce in place.)
One fell off! (I gasp in alarm.)
ONE FELL OFF! (Their concern is real.)
And bumped his head! (I grab my head.)
AND BUMPED HIS HEAD! (Their heads roll in pain.)
He went to the doctor! (I pump my arms as if running.)
HE WENT TO THE DOCTOR! (Elbows crash into elbows.)
And the doctor said, (I place my hands on my hips.)
AND THE DOCTOR SAID, (They are straining to see whom I will pick.)
You stop jumping (I lean over Laxmi, shaking a scolding finger.)
YOU STOP JUMPING! (They wag their fingers.)
On the bed!
ON THE BED! (I am hoping the gong will sound, but it doesn't.)

Now how many?

NINE!

I write s-e-v-e-n on the board, deliberately mixing the numbers.

NO! They scream.

N-i-n-e, I write.

YES!

Nine little monkeys (And, thankfully, the gong sounds.)

THANK YOU, MADAM! (They wait to see what I will say today.)

Have a nice day.

HAVE A NICE DAY! They scream, and I exit into the bright sunlight, having survived another day with fourth class.

Prayer flags at the monastery in Pokhara

4

I feel like such a sleuth. Today I actually got a good look at a green magpie, which, according to *Birds of Nepal*, is a shy bird that likes leafy cover and is hard to see.

I awoke at my regular time, but I didn't run because I am trying to change my compulsive habits. Armed with bird book and binoculars, I climbed the hill to help the Buddhists greet the sunrise. I usually see several birds on my way to the monastery, and this morning I saw an Indian pie, a cuckoo, a black and white robin dyal, and several myanas. Butterflies floated between the bushes—glassy tigers and yellow swallowtails.

I don't know how many times I've climbed the monastery hill east of my house since I came to Pokhara. Not nearly as many, of course, as the old women I followed, who fingered their beads and spun their little prayer wheels as they walked. I joined the line of worshippers, walking clockwise, spinning each bronze prayer wheel in its turn. Such a simple way to scatter good will to the wind and world. The prayer flags, one for each primary element, were waving. The yellow seemed an extra flash of morning sun, fluttering against the mountains.

From the monastery I have developed a good walking route that takes about two hours. I picked my way through some terraced fields, past a hedge row of large poinsettias and scrubby trees, and turned sharply up the hill through a ravine that probably runs like a river during monsoon. The trail leveled out for a while with nice views of the Pokhara valley.

I saw several interesting birds. They were all exciting to me, even the very common ones, like the black drongo, a large bird with a long, deeply forked tail. Perched on a bare limb was a black-headed shrike, a graceful bird with a cinnamon-colored body, a black head and tail, and a white patch on the throat and wings. The mandibles from the shrikes are used in a ritual for six-month-old babies called the "rice feeding ceremony." The child is fed rice with the mandible, which assures wisdom.

I sat down on a wall for a while, puzzling over a small crested yellow-and-black bird I had seen. I'm pretty sure it was a yellow-cheeked tit, a noisy, musical little bird, but it flitted around so quickly that I mostly saw yellow and black streaks. I'm such a novice at this. My mother loved birds. I'd look obediently when she would point them out, but I was too young then and too full of other things to share the love with her.

I felt very lazy in the sun. The terraced fields were green with the recent rains, but only an occasional mustard field actually bloomed. Across the ravine I heard a chortling kind of coo. I thought it was some kind of pigeon and considered starting toward the sound, but at that moment, a Nepali on his way up the hill to the village above stopped for conversation.

He was interested in the bird book, so I showed it to him. I managed to ask what bird we could hear and he took the question very seriously. He pored over the pictures. I was sure the bird would be long gone before I ever got over to look for it. He settled, after some deliberation, on a picture of a green magpie. He told me it would be hard to see since they are more afraid of people than other magpies. At least, that's what I think he said.

The man continued up the hill, but I went over the wall and slowly skirted the mustard field to the clump of bamboo. I didn't want to frighten the bird, so I moved slowly and didn't flash the binoculars, as the book assured me it would dash to cover amidst green foliage. When I was sure I was quite close to where the sound originated, I just waited. The call stopped. The bird flew from one bamboo stand to another, and because I had seen it land, I could look cautiously with the binoculars. Sure enough, just as the book said, the bird was bright green with rufous wings.

5

I've been tutoring Indu, a twenty-four-year-old science teacher at my school who wants to take the TOEFL exam next year. That's the Test of English as a Foreign Language, one of those Princeton-based tests of English proficiency to determine eligibility for studying abroad. Indu is convinced it's his ticket out of poverty.

We've been working through a *Barron* test preparation booklet together. I'm extremely glad I was born speaking English because I never would have mastered it as a foreign language. Much of the test is constructed around the examinee's listening to passages and conversations and interpreting what has been said. We don't have the tapes, so I read the selection aloud and we pick out confusing phrases or extreme Americanisms. Example: "I'll take the house dressing, please." You're supposed to guess—or know—that this has nothing to do with a house, a dress, or getting dressed, that the phrase, in fact, conveys that you are in a restaurant ordering a special sauce for your salad.

That phrase alone took ten minutes. Indu has never eaten at what we consider a restaurant, although there are several of them for the tourists in Pokhara. He makes only fifty dollars a month as a teacher and is the main support of his wife, baby, two unemployed brothers, and aging parents, so he couldn't possibly spend rupees on such a frivolous activity. Nepalis, that is, ordinary Nepalis like Indu, don't eat salads. They cook their vegetables. "And then you dress the salad?" he asked, baffled. But house dressing was nothing compared to MUZAK.

A fairly long selection on which several comprehension questions were based described how MUZAK, explained in one phrase as background music, is used to manipulate human behavior by something called stimulus progression. This innocuous-sounding music was of great benefit to a retail store owner, according to this narrative, because it could increase employee production output up to thirty percent. This effect was achieved by strategically increasing the tempo of the music during times when the employees would normally be slowing down. Ten-thirty a.m. and two-thirty p.m. were cited. MUZAK could also be used to manipulate consumer spending. When, for instance, slow music was played in a supermarket, the customer would push the cart more slowly and pick up more items. However, in a restaurant, if fast music was played during the lunch hour, people would eat faster, resulting in a quicker turnover of tables so more customers could be served in the same amount of time.

I finished the passage and looked up. Indu was staring at me as if I had switched from speaking English, with which he was at least minimally familiar, to a tribal dialect involving grunts and clicks. Our cultural gap had never been greater.

I started with the easiest. Background music. Nepal has plenty of music, and in Pokhara you see an occasional boom box, although for the most part radios blare out the same station as you pass the shops. I couldn't explain piped-in music, so I moved on.

Supermarket. Now Pokhara has something called, in English, the Supermarket. It's pretty amazing for Nepal, actually. It's a covered labyrinth of little shops that some entrepreneur with capital, who no doubt had seen the one on New Road in Kathmandu, has tried to copy. Three-quarters of the potential shops are empty, their corrugated front panels tightly closed. The rest are filled with an almost identical array of cheap plastic goods from India and second-line western-type clothes made in Korea and Hong Kong. These are referred to by my students as the "fancy shops." No shiny metal carts with wheels exist to push slowly through expansive aisles to dreamy music. I try to imagine MUZAK in the REAL market at Mahendra Pul in the center of town with its colorful array of vegetable stalls, woven baskets with live chickens, meat tables with severed goats' heads, and cows that capitalize on their protected status by trying to eat everyone's wares.

How do I tackle "increased employee production output"?

Work is so different here. Over ninety percent of Nepal's population is involved in agriculture. Indu's family owns a few acres on which they grow rice and corn. Most crafts are determined by hereditary caste. But jobs that pay money are hard to find. The little shops are strictly mom and pop operations with mom often sitting there breast-feeding the baby. Some people have government jobs which they can get if they have a college degree, but government employees mostly sit around all day because the capital that was needed for their projects has never materialized. Teachers, like Indu, have six classes a day with as many as eighty-five students each. Gangs of laborers, hired for specific projects, swarm over the building sites. The unemployment rate is astronomical.

I am beginning to feel sad. I don't want to talk to Indu about "increased employee output." My educated Nepali friends already exhibit an uneasiness. They have been inculcated with the idea of inferiority to westerners—perhaps because so many are here showing them how to do things the "right" way. The notion that Nepalis are lazy is distressingly pervasive. I've heard it many times—not only from westerners, but from Nepalis themselves.

I even hesitate to share a successful lesson with my teachers anymore because they're so sure I've done something better than they could ever do. My headsir inevitably throws in a remark about how American teachers work hard but Nepali teachers are lazy. No, I protest, Nepali teachers work under conditions American teachers would never accept and they do so with minimal materials and for very little money. I think Nepali teachers are doing very well. They smile and love me for saying this, but they don't believe me.

So how do I explain the idea of an employer musically manipulating his employees to work more for the same wage? I have a sudden image of the human chains passing pans of cement up the ladders in building construction projects here for less than a dollar a day. I've seen as many as thirty in a row. I picture them working in double time in the heat to a transistor radio blaring fast music.

I could try to explain "manipulated consumer spending" or the idea of "rapid turnover" during lunch hour. (Here men dawdle for hours over *chiyaa* for *gaf garne*, small talk, with friends.) But we're both tired, so I call it quits for the day and send Indu home to re-read the passage before we try to deal with the questions. For the first time I really understand the "cultural bias" of standardized tests that minority groups complain about in the States. The specifics are different here, but this test is developmentally biased against Indu. A non-native speaker of English from a developed country would have a much better chance for a high score. Not only would the words conjure up familiar images, but the morality of psychological manipulation for financial gain would be accepted without question. Life here is still too close to the reality of basic survival for that to make any sense.

I glance ahead at the next lesson. It's about a woman on a diet. That should be fun to explain in a land where to be *moto*, fat, is beautiful, because so few people can afford to be. About as much fun as trying to explain that in America people pay money to lose weight, while in Nepal people starve if the hail ruins the rice because they don't have the money to buy other food.

6

I woke up at four this morning feeling much better after a week of illness and decided I definitely had to get out of the house. I had gone to school yesterday, but was still in a fog with everything a little out of focus and the wrong color. Joy, a young teacher who is posted at the village of Saimarang about five hours northeast of Pokhara, had stayed here last night and was going to head back early, so I decided I'd go part way with her and hike back on my own.

We caught a bus down at the intersection where my running route joins the Kathmandu road, climbed on the top, and rode for about forty-five minutes to a village at the end of a lake called Begnaas Tal. For ten rupees we rode on a small boat with some Nepalis, who spoke Tamang. The ride across the lake took a pleasant half-hour. Begnaas Tal is a natural lake that has been enlarged with a dam. The eastern Annapurnas made sharp reflections in the water and fish jumped beside the boat.

Just before we started up the ridge at the end of the lake, we stopped at a *chiyaa* shop. A nice old Tamang man who had shared our boat ride insisted on paying for our tea. Upstairs in the shop two young women were weaving materials into complex geometrical patterns which involved an incredible number of spindles. This material is used in *topis*, slanted hats all the men wear.

Over the first ridge, a series of steps rose precipitously. The himals came back into sight when we crested the second ridge, and except for a few cuts that took me behind hills, the mountains were my companions the rest of the day. After about an hour and a half, Joy cut off toward Saimarang. We could see her school on the next ridge, but she still had an hour of walking up and down to get there.

According to the people in the *chiyaa* shop, I could expect a three-hour walk along the ridge to Pokhara. Three Nepali hours were easily four-and-a-half for me, for I did a lot of bird-watching and looking at the spectacular scenery. I could see the Annapurnas and Machhapuchhare and for a while the Lamjung Himal as well. Always the mountains formed a backdrop for the other vignettes: the thatched orange houses, the cascade of terraced fields down precipitous ridges, the women with clothes all shades of maroon, red, and pink, carrying brass jugs, against a deep blue sky.

I saw a pair of eagles. I never did figure out which variety they were even though they were most obliging. One sat in a tree and preened, spreading his wings so I could see the color pattern. I also saw several Egyptian vultures with their orange feathered heads, circling and circling. They are most beautiful for birds whose livelihood is such a nasty business.

By the time I started down off the ridge, I felt absolutely gluttonous with natural beauty. How rich the Nepalis are for all their lack of western wealth. I try not to overly romanticize the pastoral scene, because the elimination of the health problems in these villages would certainly add to the comfort of life for the Nepalis. But I am having a crisis of confidence about anything the developed nations have to "give" or teach Nepal about the quality of life.

I think of one village where I rested. Saturday is a *bidhaa*, holiday, in Nepal, and little clusters of men gathered lazily under the *chautaara*, the resting tree, with its gnarly roots. Little boys tossed a ball made from old socks back and forth to each other. The women at the water tap, in their wonderful wildflower shades of clothes, stood talking with their golden water urns glowing in the sun. Four little girls played a complicated jump rope game. Could I honestly say these people's lives would have been improved if they had spent their *bidhaa* at the mall?

Tamang women east of Pokhara. One gives the namaste
sign, with palms together in polite greeting.

7

I've spent all day on the roof. This is one of my favorite vantage points to view Pokhara. I started out here this morning because I needed to hang my washing to dry. The sun was so pleasant I brought my notebooks and sleeping bag and camped here all day. Now the sun has almost reached the blue hills in the west.

I washed all my clothes, including my bedding. I don't enjoy this hand laundry business. Luckily, most of my clothes are an indiscriminate shade of khaki. Actually, I'm amazed at how much white is worn here, in a land where keeping anything white is virtually impossible. Today is Saturday, and from my perch by the railing this morning I saw clothes, especially white ones, spread to dry on roof tops and bushes. On Sunday, the first day of the school week, my students appear in white shirts, blue skirts and pants, and the girls with red ribbons. Admittedly, the shirts are often dingy by Friday, but on Sunday, they are white again. I don't know how the mothers get them so clean.

The students who attend the "English Boarding Schools" (they are actually day schools) where those with money send their children instead of to the government schools where I teach, wear even more white. One of the schools that I pass each day has students in all-white uniforms. The girls wear white blouses and skirts and the boys wear white long pants. All have handkerchiefs pinned to their left shoulders. Perhaps the white represents some symbolic assault on the dust in which they live.

Most amazing of all is the fact that the children also wear white canvas shoes. This fact can only be appreciated if you are acquainted with what feet encounter here. I sometimes amuse myself imagining the responses of people who make pooper-scooper and litter laws to what I see on my daily trip between the house and school. Such a plethora of possibilities for legal action.

The white shirts have been gathered from the bushes now. What I still can see are the college students over in the big field by the Gandaki Hospital organizing a noisy rally. The political atmosphere is heating up as the scheduled elections for the legislative body approaches. No one seems quite sure exactly when they will happen. According to rumors I've heard, toward the end of April or early May we will get an extended vacation when the schools close down for students to campaign. These are the first real elections Nepal has ever had, so Nepalis are taking them quite seriously. The major parties are the Congress Party, which supports a limited monarchy, and the Communists, who want to change everything.

The majority of the people can't read and write, so the campaigning and voting is done by symbols. The symbol of the Congress party is a tree and the Communists' symbol is a sun. I made up this rhyme for my fourth class to help them make sense of all the graffiti.

This is a sun.
This is a tree.
Each one says
Please vote for me!
That is a
De- moc- ra- cy.
This is a sun.
This is a tree.

I wish it were that simple. More parties surface every day. I've heard forty-seven in all are registered. The other symbols painted everywhere are a cow and a plough. I'm losing patience with having everything, including our new upper school building, splashed with paint. All the parties, of course, are starting to fight with each other and yell conflicting slogans. Actually, it's rather a blessing not to be able to understand most of what they're saying. But it's not too hard to imagine. The cadences of the students' chants floating across the field have a depressingly familiar ring.

Other scenes in the neighborhood are more interesting to me than a western-style political rally. Across the lane, the row of red clay houses where the *saano chaat*, lowest caste, live has been in an uproar of dancing the last few days because someone is getting married. With evening coming, the people have gathered for another night of merriment. In the golden light all the neighborhood children are beginning to dance in the street. By the canal something catches my eye that reminds me of the magnolia trees in Oregon with their large white blossoms. The white blossoms on the tree are really cattle egrets, and as I watch, more and more birds land, until the tree is in full bloom with large white flowers.

Across the duck stream on the other side of the house, two old *hajaraamaas*, grandmothers, permanently bent forward from carrying the *dokos*, baskets with the straps, across their foreheads, hobble along, their shawls drawn up over their heads. A blue Indian roller with his lovely two-toned turquoise wings swoops back and forth in the last shafts of the sun. Now, just as the light begins to fade, the egrets rise, as if a signal has been given. They curve in formation against the purple clouds, their legs behind them, catching the sun.

8

Most of the time Nepal seems like a magical kingdom with friendly people who live simple lives, fulfilling basic human needs. But living on a daily basis with the real live people here is sometimes more of a strain than my idyllic descriptions convey.

Part of the strain is that I am beginning to be more cognizant of the underlying current of resentment toward development workers. It is one thing to recognize the validity of that resentment intellectually and quite another to deal with it on a human level. Just yesterday when I found that I had actually said the Nepali equivalent of "eat shit" to a little kid on my walk home from school, it seemed time to regroup my thoughts about this experience.

Actually, the remark came out of a conversation with my friend Dorothy, who has been in Nepal for twenty-seven years and has established a natural history museum on the college campus in Pokhara. She is a modest, soft-spoken woman not at all given to that sort of unrefined conversation. We were talking about trekking. I asked her if after twenty-seven years she still got the annoying "Hello Mister one rupee" routine from children. She said yes but she mostly ignored it. What she really didn't like was when kids said "Hell-o-*kaaka-dello*," which is something you hear a lot around Pokhara. I was surprised because it's said in a lilting little sing-song that doesn't sound offensive. She informed me that the *kaakadello* part is a slang word for a big runny *"disaa"* like *bisee* poop, and the phrase is used derogatorily toward westerners.

So what did she do when she heard it, I asked, for I have heard it many times from children playing in full view of their parents who obviously would know the connotations of the phrase. I was suddenly uncomfortable about them laughing behind my back when I smiled at the children. She said she simply acted puzzled and turned to ask the child whether he ate *kaakadello* as if she were confused about the meaning. I thought of the phrase and started to laugh because if you said *"kaakadello khannchau"* without the question mark, you would be literally saying "eat *bisee* poop." It was this innocuous exchange that laid the basis for my cultural insensitivity.

Sometimes I'm unsure I'm serving any constructive purpose here. In fact, one could argue that emphasizing English in a nation that has yet to sort out its options for modernizing both its economy and governmental structure smacks of an outdated imperialistic concept of where the real source of advanced ideas is located. That troubling notion has been festering in my mind, so no doubt the nagging guilt that accompanies it contributed to my uncharitable remark yesterday.

I was coming home when it happened. The day had been so crazy at school with rain drumming on the tin roof and adding to the usual din of sixty-plus fourth class students squashed together. The noise of the sixth class came over the partition. The heavy clouds made it too dark in the unlighted room for the kids to see the picture and story I'd made on brown mail wrapper paper for them to copy. "Pandemonium" is too mild a word to describe the noise. The whole row of classrooms throbbed with similar sound.

I walked out in the rain when the gong sounded, glad to have escaped. By the time I was halfway to the house, the sun was back out in a steamy haze and people were outside again. I walked through Mahendra Pul and right before I crossed the bridge to start out to MatePani, a little kid who was sitting beside a vegetable cart said in a sing-song, "Hell-o-*kaaka-dello.*" And without even thinking, I answered in a similar singsong, *"kaaka-dello khannchau."* He looked very surprised and ducked behind the cart.

Now I don't suppose there's a reason to feel proud in any culture about having told a smart-alec kid such a thing, but I'm not going to dredge up any artificial guilt either. When I got back to the house I took off my skirt, made up a cup of coffee and a peanut butter sandwich, and retreated under the mosquito net over my mattress on the floor with a photograph album of home. I looked for a long time at the pictures of the backyard with the dogwood tree and the crabapple tree in bloom.

I know why I came here—and fortunately only one part of it was that need to plug into the larger world picture by giving something. For I have come to understand that there isn't very much of ourselves or the positive things in our culture that we can give away. When I feel like this I have to focus on the self-serving reason I came—to redefine my own personal and societal values by living in another culture—because that need is being met. So in a personal way the experience is worthwhile. But I'm not harboring any false illusions about how much benefit the Third World is getting from all the "development" aid, financial and human, that flows from the industrialized societies.

We in the developed world would like to believe we have something to give. In a letter I received last week, one of the young teachers at my school in Portland described feeling terribly depressed over the Gulf situation and how our society had unleashed all that destruction. I know he needed to believe that people like me who are "giving" something could in some small way be a counterbalance. So when he thanked me for "doing more for humankind than hundreds of millions of others even think of doing," he wasn't just being naive and melodramatic. I know him well, and he's a particularly practical and realistic young man. He knows I'm not really giving much. He'd probably even think my woeful story of how little I gave yesterday was funny. I think he just wished when he wrote, that we would, at least, do no harm.

The negative things from the industrialized societies reach the developing world in abundance: the plastic bags, the expired drugs, the carcinogenic products deemed unfit for consumption in the first world, and always the weapons.

Good things from the industrialized world—like access to free education, affordable medical care, and participatory governments—seem to work well only when they have been homegrown. The other day as I was standing on my roof, I watched a Nepali man turning the earth with his team of oxen and his wooden plough. His wife followed, scattering the seeds by hand in the furrows.

So much development aid has been pouring into Nepal—an inundation of mostly good intentions—and much of it has run off like the early spring thundershowers, noisy and colorful, but with little substance. The positive aspects of modernization that will really grow and flourish here will have to come from that pair of farmers after they have prepared the ground for the natural monsoon. And their societies will be so much richer for finding ways to modernize that are compatible with their indigenous traditions.

I don't blame the Nepalis for an ambivalent attitude toward development workers who have succeeded mostly in giving the more educated a vague sense of unease and inferiority and the feeling that they should spend less time singing, dancing, and enjoying their families, and more time trying to acquire material goods. But that doesn't mean I have to let a little kid call me *bisee* poop either. I'll get out the Nepali dictionary and figure out a more culturally sensitive reply.

VI

THE CLIMB TO THE MARDI HIMAL

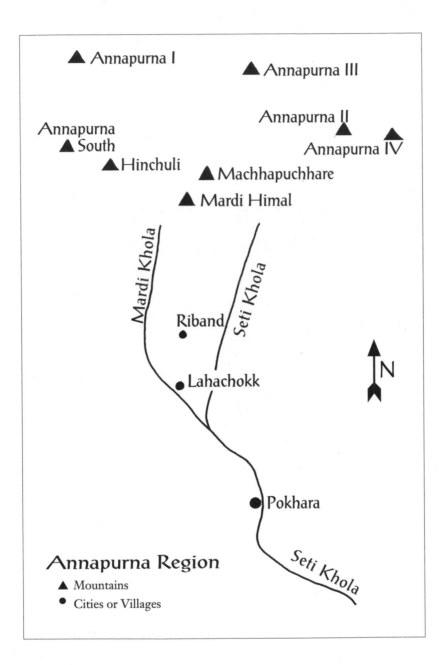

▲ Annapurna I

▲ Annapurna III

Annapurna II

Annapurna
▲ South

▲ Annapurna IV

▲ Hinchuli

▲ Machhapuchhare

▲ Mardi Himal

Mardi Khola

Seti Khola

Riband
●

Lahachokk
●

N

● Pokhara

Annapurna Region
▲ Mountains
● Cities or Villages

Seti Khola

Pokhara
March

Notice that I say, "the climb to." That is because we never reached Mardi Himal, although we did get close enough to see the silver slabs of glacier clinging to slopes too steep even to hold snow. So this isn't going to be a story of triumph and heroic flag planting. But that doesn't matter. I've been on enough summits, and I didn't have much investment in reaching this one. I just wanted to climb high in the Himalayas.

Mardi Himal was another of the beautiful surprises of Nepal. I had started taking yoga lessons from a lovely young woman named Lydia. We warmed to each other immediately, and one Saturday I hiked with her to Lahachokk, the village where her husband David was working on research for his Ph.D. dissertation. As we rode on the top of the bus to the trailhead that started up to Lahachokk, Lydia showed me the Mardi Himal, a jagged thrust on the west ridge of Machhapuchhare. She told me David had wanted to climb, but the plan was looking shaky because the man he had arranged to climb with had backed out, and the peak permit and guide were too expensive for just one. It was a ready-made plan for action, and I couldn't believe my luck.

In the States I probably wouldn't ask to miss school to climb a mountain. For one thing, it would cost me hundreds of dollars in unpaid leave. Here teachers only make about fifty dollars a month anyway. And for another, my school district at home probably wouldn't consider mountain climbing a valid reason to be gone.

But when I asked my headsir, Hem Rej Regme, he never batted an eye. Somebody is always gone from school for some reason. In a country where distance is still measured by walking hours, even attending a meeting can mean being gone for a week. It's getting too hot to study anyway. In a week or so we'll go on morning schedule (6 a.m. to 10 a.m.), with all classes abbreviated to half-an-hour. And in May, Nepal will hold its first democratic elections. This generates so much excitement that the schools project closing for fifteen to twenty days. I rather like this approach. My own protestant work ethic hounds me less and less the longer I live in this culture.

So I was perfectly happy to take a week off to climb Mardi Himal. I knew the weather was getting marginal for good climbing. Heavy spring snow had fallen in the mountains. Even if we had reached the summit of Mardi Himal at 18,222 feet, we would have achieved only a little bump on the west ridge of Machhapuchhare (23,000 feet). Behind that are the Annapurnas (26,000 feet). One of the lessons I've learned in Nepal is that success is relative to the Himalayan proportions of the task. You might as well take enough time to enjoy the rhododendrons on the way.

▲

Day 1

The guide, Salakpa Sherpa, and his assistant Pemba rode the night bus from Kathmandu. They hired two more porters in Pokhara, and David and I met them at noon at the Bag Bazaar near the old Shining Hospital. I had a strange, nervous time the evening before. Even though I insisted to myself that I was acting silly, because I had no premonition of disaster, I straightened my meager little room of belongings, neatly arranging all my clothes in the small tin trunks.

We all took a jeep from the Bag Bazaar to the trailhead. After about a mile of walking we crossed a suspension bridge over the Mardi Khola and stopped briefly to rest in the cool shade before we climbed the steep steps up the side of the gorge. A *doko*, a large cone-shaped basket, lay on its side in the sun, with four puppies using it to play hide-and-seek.

We climbed for an hour to reach Lahachokk, an especially charming village with several circular orange houses. The Annapurnas tower over the plateau above the river where Lahachokk begins. David pointed out the high caste Brahmin section farther up the hill, but we proceeded to the lower Gurung section. There we all stopped for tea at the place where David and Lydia rent a room above a *bisee* stall. I had met the *aamaa*

Aamaa *chopping firewood at Lahachokk*

the last time I had visited the village. She was a lovely wrinkled woman whose dignity was only slightly lessened by the Michael Jackson bandana on her head. She nervously cautioned David about the climb, obviously a little uneasy about my part in it.

We continued climbing the hill to the Gurung village of Riband and camped in a terraced field for the night. David had engaged Ganeshko Baa, which means Ganesh's father, to meet us there. Ganeshko Baa is a herder, familiar with the high slopes, who was hired to accompany us to the base camp and show us where to find water. Mardi Himal is infrequently climbed and not on a trekking route. The only available description, taken from a 1961 climb account, noted a paucity of water and difficulty in locating the route.

On the way to Riband I'd seen the *Datura*, the white trumpet flower vine that is a powerful hallucinogenic and sacred to Shiva. Before we set up the tent on an unplanted terraced field, we stopped again for tea with a family David knew. The *hajaraamaa* wore four large gold rings in the rims of her ears that bent them forward, and the lobes hung elongated like small trumpet flowers. The tent fascinated the children of the village and they lined up before the flap, perched on their heels. We could see the lights of Pokhara below the blue layers of terraced fields as the stars came out over the curve of the hills.

▲

Day 2

We started from Riband before eight. The children had already gathered to look in the tent, but when we took it down they went off to play their game of shot put with stones. We saw people from the village gathering firewood. Each family has certain areas from which they are allowed to take the dead wood without a permit.

Birds and flowers dominated the day. The lower rhododendrons had finished blooming so we walked through a carpet of reddish-brown fallen blossoms. Cascades of fragrant white orchids, *coelogyne cristata*, hung in the chestnut trees. The first wild strawberry blossoms that would turn into veritable dancing meadows appeared along the trail.

Ganeshko Baa found water. We stopped so the Nepalis could make *daal bhaat* for their morning meal. David and I ate bread and peanut butter and looked for birds. We saw a pair of scarlet minavets. The porters and guides joked and talked. When Salakpa asked Ganeshko Baa what work his son Ganesh did, he said, *"Ke kaam?"* What work? The discontent of young men in the villages is legendary. Ganesh has been to Hong Kong, and David surmised he might be a gold smuggler. The son who goes off to seek his fortune and brings back riches for the family is an enduring theme in Nepali media. Often there is a sad ending, in both the stories and reality. Horror stories abound of Nepali workers in Indian coal mines or factory workers in Korea who are kept in boxcars. Finally David and I continued walking, as the *bhaat* procedure was a lengthy one, indeed, with a huge kettle of rice and the *daal* still bubbling.

As we gained altitude, rhododendrons still bloomed. Vivid pink blossoms were interspersed with the deep red ones. We could hear thunder rumbling from Annapurna South across the Mardi Khola.

A soft rain started, like Oregon rain. When it gained force, we opened the black umbrellas everyone uses in Nepal. I put on my slicker. The porters spread sheets of plastic over the baskets they carried by forehead straps. I saw a beautiful blue niltava with a red breast in a bush protected from the rain. Jack-in-the-pulpits trembled with raindrops in the roots of trees and under bushes. In places they grew thickly like trillium in early May around the Mt. Hood cabin at home.

We emerged from the trees onto a ridge. The rain had stopped. A large stand of jack-in-the-pulpits glistened; I counted forty-three. On the side of the hill a magnolia tree with large lotus-like white blossoms quivered in the sudden sun. A hollow jangling bell sounded in the distance from a *bisee* left to forage.

Ganeshko Baa wanted to camp at a spot with water, so we continued through the enchanted forest of thirty- to forty-foot-high rhododendron trees. Moss covered the branches and vines hung in long ropes. The light in the forest was soft and green.

We camped at 9,700 feet near a set of pastures known as Kumaii. A large pink rhododendron tree stood in bloom against Annapurna

II and IV and the Lamjung Himal in the distance. Himalayan sun-
birds with their golden breasts were feeding in the blossoms. The
wind stirred suddenly. The mountains glowed pink, then turned
to a charcoal sketch.

We talked for quite a while that night. David and Lydia are
Buddhists and attend meditative retreats. David described some
of the teachings of the Dalai Lama, who has simplified much of
the complexity of Buddhism to basic rules of compassion—that
all people want happiness and don't want suffering, so we should
act accordingly. The war and strife in the world are bad karma
playing itself out and can be understood by listening to the sounds
of the slaughterhouse at midnight.

I lay awake a long time, thinking of what he had said.

▲

Day 3

We rose early and the milky swirls of the clouds indicated the
day would not stay clear. We soon gained elevation and began
to pass more rhododendron trees in bloom. When we reached a
high plateau with a little tarn, the porters wanted to stop for *bhaat*.
They gathered wood and built a fire. The wind blew colder and
the sky looked like rain. I put on my climbing boots as I knew
we would soon be walking in snow. I wandered off to watch birds
by the tarn and saw a flock of altai accentors, greyish brown with
mottled breasts. The rain began, so David and I started climbing
the ridge to keep warm and soon the others finished *bhaat* and
followed.

The rain changed to wet flakes. We began walking on snow,
and the steepness of the ridge made it a third-class climb. My gloves
were soon soaked. Ganeshko Baa led us to a rock shelter on the
side of the ridge where we hovered against the wall. He was
shivering. He wore an oblong piece of wool pointed in a hood.
David gave him a jacket. Proper equipment and clothing for
guides and porters present a problem. People desperately need
work so they will say they have warm clothes for climbing on the
snow even when they don't have them. At least our porters and
guides all had shoes.

When the snow lightened we continued. We toiled up the ridge, kicking snow steps because the trail had become obscured. I found myself relying on dubious grass handholds, tough grass like the pampas grass in Peru. I could see large bird tracks but no birds. David saw an Impeyan pheasant with an iridescent blue back and called out, but I missed it.

When we topped the ridge, the sun came out. The snow was soft and deep and the light startlingly bright. We were missing one porter. Salakpa didn't seem worried, but I was. I had no idea how they could balance those heavy *dokos*, baskets. I had trouble with just a day pack. (Later we found out the porter had fallen, and it had taken him an hour to catch us.) It was warm and pleasant on the ridge top. The clouds swirled around Annapurna II and IV, breaking to show the peaks, then settling again. The others walked ahead. I enjoyed the sun. Only the porter who had fallen was behind me.

Ganeshko Baa insisted we drop to a scrubby rhododendron forest to camp. The snow was not packed, and I sunk past my knees. When I reached the camp, the porters were building a fire. Ganeshko Baa was gathering firewood in his bare feet in the snow. The sunshine felt warm as we watched the rain falling in blue-sheeted lines below us in the Pokhara valley. The altitude was approximately 12,000 feet.

▲

Day 4

We rose at five to break camp. Ganeshko Baa, a dignified, quiet man with a lined face, started down. He directed us to the last livestock corral, which was as high as the porters would go.

Annapurna South loomed to the left as we crested the ridge. The snow crust held at times, but when we broke through, we sunk to our thighs. David and Salakpa led. Many three-toed pheasant tracks crisscrossed the snow in patches. I became obsessed with seeing one and stopped to watch and listen. Once when I stopped, I heard a dull thudding that sounded like the beginning of the whirring thump the grouse make by our cabin. I realized after I stopped that it was my heart. *"Bistaari, bistaari,"* I reminded myself to go slowly at that altitude. I came to a place where the pheasants had been feeding. Many of the large-toed tracks circled where they had scratched away a patch of snow to feed.

By nine-thirty we arrived at the last corral where we would make base camp. It seemed such a waste of good climbing time on a clear day to stop so soon, but Salakpa said it was better to adjust to the altitude. The next day he, David, and I would get up early when the snow was hard and climb to make a high camp. The day after that we would try to climb the peak. As we rested in the sun before organizing our gear, a beautiful Impeyan pheasant, the national bird of Nepal, flew low over the ridge before us, veering off in startled surprise. It was iridescent blue, with a white patch on its back and a tan tail. Soon after, large Himalayan griffons began to circle, eyeing us curiously. Their shadows floated back and forth across the snow, and butterflies, black, white, brown, and yellow, danced in the sun.

While we were sitting there, David told me of a strange recurring dream he has had—that Lydia tells him she no longer loves him and he becomes violent. They have been through troubled times, but he loves her dearly and now they want a child. The dream frightens him, almost as much for the violence as for losing Lydia. I told him I could relate to the fear, for I think many times of how painful it would be if I spent this time away from Jim realizing how much he means to me only to find that he had realized instead that I am superfluous in his life. But I could not relate to the violence. It was useless to dwell on the fear of loss. He could lose Lydia in spite of anything he might do. Love ebbs and flows and circumstances and events can complicate the best of relationships. But if that happened, he would survive, because all of us do. He should try to let go of the fear and concentrate instead on his own potential for violence. He smiled and called me a wise old lady. I felt a surge of warmth for this young man who reminded me so much of my own tall sons.

We spent the afternoon organizing our gear for the high camp. David was a little worried about Salakpa's casual approach to equipment, and he rigged up prussicks and slings. I was worried about carrying too much, but I felt it was necessary to do my share. The day stayed sunny until about three o'clock, when the clouds boiled up to obscure the sun. Salakpa and Pemba put up a pole

with Buddhist prayer flags. Salakpa burned juniper
a *mantra*. The wind blew harder. The flags flutt
scattering their prayers to the mountains for a safe cl

▲

Day 5

We rose at two-thirty, but it still took until after four to leave
camp. The sky was beautifully clear with the band of the Milky
Way very distinct and the white hump of Annapurna South showing
in the starlight. Just as we started we saw a shooting star. The
ascent to the ridge was much harder than I anticipated. A thin
layer of snow clung to the steep ridge. Where steps could be cut,
the footing felt more secure, although I didn't like high-angle climbing with my heavy pack. I had the first of what would be many
waves of fear as I felt the weight shift on my back. I had a sudden flash of a fall I took in December while hiking the trail from
the Annapurna Sanctuary. The weight of my pack had literally
flipped me head over heels to roll down the hill. A fall from this
ridge would offer scant chance of a good story later.

The first crest of the ridge offered a brief reprieve with a fairly
level walk across a snowfield. The sun was beginning to strike
the faces of Annapurna and Machhapuchhare, creating a spectacular view. The Mardi Himal showed sheer glaciated couiers, bare
ice, too steep for even the snow to cling. The route described in
the book started on the back side of Mardi Himal, toward
Machhapuchhare. Salakpa was worried. He was not sure we had
come up the right ridge. He said our chances for success didn't
look promising because of the recent heavy snow. He was afraid
we would need technical ice equipment. I kept silent, but David,
thank god, said we'd keep an open mind, that we weren't tied to
that particular peak and just wanted to get some really good views.
I was already worried about coming down the ridge we had just
ascended with my heavy pack. I mentally resolved to ask to have
it lowered on the rope.

We continued along the ridge. At times the exposure was high,
but the footing on the snow was good. On one sharp incline I
sunk suddenly in snow to my thigh. David and Salakpa were far
ahead. I could not lift my foot. For several minutes I chopped

the snow around my leg to release it. I moved carefully, trying not to twist my knee. I felt as if I had already climbed Mt. Hood, not from tiredness, but from tension. I wanted Jim. I trusted him in front of me. I didn't really know these men.

As we leveled on a short ridge, we sat for a few minutes. A decision had to be made about Mardi Himal. Salakpa scanned the scene. He would, he said, recommend against it. It would take two more days of climbing, and he did not feel we had adequate equipment. Both David and I readily agreed to change the plan. I would gladly have turned around. I was higher than I ever expected to be, had seen an incredible sunrise, and had a gnawing fear about the descent.

David and Salakpa decided to top the ridge and make a decision on where to camp. It was a steep hump, with an icy chute for the route. No one mentioned the rope. I suggested they go on and I would wait until they decided before I came up with my pack. They went on ahead. I felt a little giddy and relieved. The sun shimmered on Annapurna South and the Nilgiris behind it. I had never been in a more beautiful spot. I dug out a chocolate bar and watched them climb. They were chopping steps in the icy chute and moving slowly. I turned away and watched the blue mist on the faraway valleys. I could see one tiny village on the side of a hill. The base camp tent was small and orange. I tried to see the prayer flags Salakpa had put up, but we were too far away.

David motioned for me to come. I was suddenly very afraid. Why were we not roped on such a high, exposed place? Because then we would all fall, since there was no way for the others to hold the weight. My mind balked. If we had decided not to climb Mardi Himal, why were we taking unnecessary risks now? But I could not go back alone. I felt a wave of fear again, then got hold of myself as David continued motioning. I put my pack on a rock and knelt beside it to get it on my back. I was glad I had cleaned my room before we came.

The first part was the worst, even though they had kicked good steps. The snow was deep and I could sink my ice ax in. Then the chute leveled a bit but the wind was blowing hard. A high

Crossing an avalanche field

rock protruded with no room to go around. I couldn't see where
they had put their feet. I made a tentative move. My pack swung
me to the right. I stepped back down, my glance catching the runout
of the fall, and my stomach tightened. Salakpa appeared at the
top of the rock. He extended his ice ax. I shook my head. I wanted
him to take the pack. He pulled it up and anchored it, then offered me the ax again. Using it as a hand hold, I pulled myself
up over the rock. I had been thoroughly shaken, and my heart
was pounding as we topped the ridge.

David was putting on crampons. The other side of the ridge
dropped sharply to a bowl and then rose several hundred feet to
a saddle. The plan, David said, was to drop to the bowl and then
climb to the saddle for a camp. In the morning we could climb
one of the rocky peaks for good views to the east. I protested.
Already we'd gone far beyond my comfort zone for risk. We were
climbing with no protection and very high exposure. The descent
into the bowl was extremely steep with the slopes on the other
side likely avalanche areas, and the sun was on the snow. Both
men were quiet. I tried to quell the panic I felt. Salakpa knew
delicacy was required. He had a frightened old lady and a strong
young man who had just had to give up the idea of Mardi Himal.
"I think, *memsahib*, this not so difficult," he said. I glared at him.
Men always think the issue is difficulty. Most climbers die from
lack of judgement, not lack of courage. I knew an avalanche slope
when I saw it. Lamely I mentioned the rope again. David knew I
would go now, so he insisted it was my decision. I began to put
on my crampons. I had climbed in more difficult places.

We started down the slope. The snow clumped under the
crampons in rounded balls. Each step required a smack with the
ice ax to render the crampons effective again. I tried not to think
about the avalanche factor. We laboriously crossed the bowl and
started up the saddle. The sun was very hot on the snow. Once
across the bowl I felt safer than I had felt all day. Salakpa came
back for my pack for the last fifteen minutes up to the saddle. I
climbed very slowly and my heart quieted.

▲

Day 6

Sometimes I just don't want to explain my reaction to men, so when the tears streamed down my face in frozen lines as we topped the ridge, I lagged behind even though I wasn't winded from the climb. The sun hovered behind the Lamjung Himal, making a golden rim along the endless line of Himalayas to the east. Already the very top of the pyramid of Machhapuchhare was catching the light, and the glaciated lines across its face were silver seams. Over the crest of one snow ridge left to climb glowed Annapurna South and the Nilgiris, close enough so the huge ice fall of the Hunchuli rippled in large crevasses like rumpled foil.

We had left our sleeping bags a little after four so we could climb the smaller peak slightly to the south of Mardi Himal. It was very cold but clear. I had not slept well, for the first time feeling the altitude. I woke several times panting for breath as if I had not been getting enough oxygen in my lungs. All three of us slept in the tent. Salakpa told us about his family in Solu Khumbu, about his four daughters and one son. He had tried to convince his villagers to bring in pipe for running water, but they had not been interested until he brought in the pipe for his own house. He had taken one daughter with him to Kathmandu for two years at boarding school so she would learn English, but she had been lonely for the family. He let her return to the village. Last year Salakpa had climbed Annapurna IV with a Canadian expedition. Next year he is scheduled for Manaslu and in 1992 for Mt. Everest. Two guides from the Sherpa Co-op Trekking Company died last year, one on Dalhigiri with two Americans and the other after he had returned to Kathmandu after a climb, maybe from drinking, Salakpa said.

We did not carry packs for this climb. When it was just beginning to get light, we started up the slope. The steps that Salakpa and David made were easy to follow. We moved slowly up the last ridge. It was very steep and had I been given a choice, I would have preferred a rope. The run-out was thousands of feet, and even if it was unobstructed snow, surely one could not survive the friction of so long a slide.

*Salakpa Sherpa on the climb to
the Mardi Himal*

We could see now the route up the back side of the Mardi Himal. It would have taken another day and would have been a hard climb. I had no regrets, but I could feel David looking at it with longing. That, I decided, was the difference between a young man and a middle-aged woman.

I felt I was held in the very palm of the sacred Machhapuchhare, and on either side the Annapurnas glistened in the early morning sun. This was the most incredible mountain experience of my life. Salakpa, with his orange-red down parka exactly like Jim's, stood facing the mountains. I felt a profound loneliness. I met Jim climbing Mount St. Helens before it erupted, and I was here now because of his love and support. More than I have ever wanted anything, I wanted him with me.

We started down the steep slope. The snow was too hard to plunge step, so we moved sideways, using our ice axes as additional holds. I was afraid, but quietly so, and kept looking to the east where the high peaks stretched as far as I could see.

When we reached the high camp, we took down the tent and packed for the descent. I dreaded this, but the sun was not yet on the avalanche fields and I knew the snow slope we had descended the day before would be easier going up. As we crossed the bowl, I appraised the situation. I had not overreacted. It was precipitously steep and a fall would mean certain death. But going up I focused my gaze intently on each step ahead of me and could not see the line of the slope trailing off into the blue haze. When I reached the crest, David and Salakpa were discussing whether to fix a belay for the steepest part of the ridge. I kept silent. They decided against it, for it would take a long time and the snow would soon begin to soften. Salakpa read my face. "I will go in front of you," he said. All that meant was that he thought I would not fall, for if I fell, I would take him, too.

We started down. It was easier with crampons and my jaw relaxed. Then we reached the rock I had faltered on before. Salakpa peered over it. I stood several feet back. He apparently decided there was no way of getting me over it and backtracked to where I was standing. "We go around," he said. "Follow my steps." To go around was to stand at the very top of a snow slab, slightly pulled away from the rock that looked positively vertical for hundreds of feet. Salakpa moved slowly. I wanted to say no, but as he continued to move farther away from me, my mind focused on a Nepali woman David and I had seen on the first day hiking up to Lahachokk. She had been standing on the side of the cliff above the confluence of the Mardi Khola and the Seti Khola, gathering fodder. From the path it looked as if she were suspended in the air, and we had to look over the side to see her standing on thin nubbins of rock as she gathered the sparse grass to put in the basket slung from her forehead with a strap. A fall would have meant sudden death on the boulders far below. The danger I was paying hundreds of dollars to experience was for her a way of life. I moved slowly in the steps Salakpa had made.

Later, on the giddy safety of the flat snow field, David pointed out the flaming red of the rhododendrons still in bloom below us in the highest forest. The Himalayan griffons hovered above us. The snow was beginning to soften in the sun. When we reached the camp, Pemba had already set up the tent to dry and the tea was boiling.

We spread out wet clothes and boots in the warm sun. I took a little of the snow water they had melted and washed my hair. Salakpa sat by the fire, bent over paper, writing. One of the porters, who could not read and write, was dictating a letter for his family. Salakpa would deliver it to the porter's home village when he had a chance to return to Solu Khumbu in eastern Nepal. I moved in slower and slower motion and finally just sat on a rock to watch the griffons floating in lazy circles on the thermal drafts. The prayer flags on the pole waved gently in the wind.

Prayer flags on a roof below Tamserku, in the
Solu Khumbu region

VII

THE HOUSE WHERE GOD LIVES

Sixth class, Byndabasini School

1

Pokhara
April

I returned to school today after my brief vacation for the Mardi Himal climb, and we were all glad to see each other. My Nepali teacher friends looked with fascination at my sunburned, peeling face. I thought Nepalis would never burn because of their dark skin, but Salakpa Sherpa, the guide we had hired, had a distinctly two-toned face from wearing snow goggles so much of his life. The teachers asked about the snow. Only the ones from the high villages have actually been on snow. The idea of deliberately sleeping on it amazed them. They retold the story to each other. To the children I was quite a hero. The fourth class and I wrote the following story, which they copied from the board into their notebooks and took home to read to their *bahinis* and *baais*, little sisters and brothers.

This is the teacher. The teacher is climbing a mountain. The mountain is big. This is snow. The snow is on the mountain. This is a tent. The teacher is sleeping in the tent.

They loved it. Every teacher should have it this easy. I've discovered in Nepal how amazingly intelligent children are. A child can emerge from a little house of orange clay where she shares a straw mat with her four sisters, come to school in a white blouse that her mother has scrubbed clean under the central water tap, sit on a bench with an impossible number of other little girls, and answer my questions politely in English, which is her THIRD language. She speaks Gurung at home and Nepali in school. After twenty-five years of trying to entertain the media-dulled youth of America, this is humbling indeed.

I could cite countless examples of the incredible cleverness of the children, from complicated games with stones (instead of Nintendos) to child care of the very young by those still young themselves. I'll give just one illustration. Bicycles. No miniature bicycles and training wheels here, only the large, gangly, universally green Chinese models. Children ride them anyway, ingeniously putting one leg under the crossbar and balancing that way. They ride all over Pokhara at what seems to be considerable risk to life and limb through streets cluttered with vegetable carts, cows, and honking taxis. I once saw a little boy riding on a bike twice his size, no doubt headed for the family market stall, with eighteen (I counted) live chickens suspended upside down by their legs from various bicycle parts.

Today was also my first day of school on morning hours. I have to be at school at six a.m., and I am all finished by ten o'clock. Such a deal. I love going through the main part of town, Mahendra Pul, while the cows are still sleeping under the overhangs in front of the closed shops. The women are already sweeping their porches and putting on the fresh layer of *bisee* dung and orange clay. Sleepy children are being hustled out of the little houses toward the school. I feel a great kinship. In the hushed half-light of morning, we are all mothers.

Mother and daughters

2

My name is Astha. I am a student. I am from Nepal. I live in Pokhara. I have got one brother. His name is Ashish. I have got one father and I have got one mother. My schools name is Bindabasini Mabi. I read in six class. My English teacher name is Barbara. She from Amarica. I like my English teacher. She love me. I like her teaching very much. I like to go to movei at Saturday. I like movei very much. I have got friends. I get up at five o'clock and come to school.

Byndabasini School, which serves
1,000 children

3

It seems impossible that I could drink a cup of coffee in this heat, but I'm fixing one. I would sell body and soul for a refrigerator. It would take them both, too. I looked in the one store in Mahendra Pul that has refrigerators, and a tiny one costs over seven hundred dollars. That's well over three times the average yearly income for a Nepali, so neither I nor most of them will get one. The temperature isn't too high—around ninety. But the haze presses down like a soft golden thumb and traps the heat. I'm glad we went on morning hours with school. The air is still fairly cool when we start, but by the time I walk home across town at ten-thirty, the heat has begun. By afternoon sounds seem to vanish completely.

Today, after I woke from my nap, I went downstairs to the water storage tank behind the house. I decided to squander a bucket of water for a bath. The water main has been closed for two days. The *hajaraamaas*, grandmothers, of the neighborhood were sleeping, stretched out on the porch on straw mats, three of them together.

I love these old women, especially our *hajaraamaa*, who is Chanda's mother-in-law. She's always dressed in maroon velvet with a wide shawl over her shoulders, which she uses to carry Biswas. Even in the heat, only her feet are bare. Six-month-old Biswas must have been inside sleeping, for when he's awake, he is attached to her back. When we meet, she always brings his little hands up in a *namaste* for me. Then she and I jabber comfortably to each other and smile. She speaks only Gurung and I alternate between Nepali and English. Of course we have absolutely no idea what the other is saying, but that doesn't hinder our mutual admiration in the least.

This whole family is a microcosm of the changing Nepal. Chanda's husband Bohj is home on leave now. He has been in Saudi Arabia as an ambulance driver for the Gurkha regiment. Chanda watched the news on her sister's TV every night during the Gulf War, hoping that she might see him. He is here for a month and brought back money. He put ceiling fans in several rooms in the house. This is wonderful when the electricity works, which it hasn't for two days. He says if he gets a promotion next year, he can take Chanda and the boys back to Hong Kong. He wears western jeans and a T-shirt but walks right in without knocking, just like other Nepalis.

I certainly can't say I'd encourage mercenary soldiering, but I have to admit this is one of the positive ways change and "development" are coming to Nepal. Chanda shows the effects of having lived in Hong Kong. Her place is scrupulously clean (her baby wears diapers), and she has four-year-old Bisal in some sort of private preschool. Every chance she gets she trots him out to recite his numbers in English or to say "good morning." All of this wealth is beyond any but the lucky few who were chosen by the British to serve in the army. They are all from the Gurung or Magar castes, which causes resentment from the higher caste Brahmins and Chhetris.

And yet, our place is home to more typical Nepalis too, who come from the Gurung village about six hours walk away, where the family lived before the present affluence. The women who come squat comfortably on their heels on the front porch and talk. Chanda serves tea on her dishes from Hong Kong. I wonder if our *bajaraamaa* gets lonesome for the village. That idea is obviously too complicated for us to discuss with smiles and gestures, so I'll never know for sure. But she seems fairly happy here.

And even though I miss Jim, so am I. I may have realized just how much our relationship provides a foundation for my emotional well-being, but I've also realized that it is actually possible to cut loose and form my own little island, as some of the women around me have done, by chance or by choice. I really needed to know that. I never was sure before that I could do it, and now I am. The amazing thing is that standing back and seeing the gossamer strands of the emotional web we have chosen to weave with our marriage makes me regard it with great tenderness and new respect.

A violent thunderstorm from the south erupted a few minutes ago, which is the first for the season. Apparently, when the storms come consistently from the south, it means the monsoon has started. That should be a month away. Right now, even though it is raining hard here, the clouds are tilted and I can see quite far up the slopes of Machhapuchhare to the north. The sun is breaking through the clouds. From the east porch I see a rainbow playing with the prayer flags on the monastery hill. Such a beautiful place to be alone.

4

Down on the Terai somewhere are the only thirty-one miles of train track in Nepal. Given that fact, perhaps "Five Hundred Miles" wasn't the best choice of songs to teach my sixth class today, but my students like to learn songs with English words. I try to sing through a new song when they're working on writing something so the tune will be familiar when I teach the words. I did that in sixth class this morning with "Five Hundred Miles." It occurred to me with a sudden rush of sadness that except for "you can hear the whistle blow" the song contains a lot of Nepali elements. The verse "not a shirt on my back, not a penny to my name—Lord, I can't go a-home this a-way" could have been part of a conversation I had with my teacher friend Indu yesterday. He was telling me that many Nepalis go out of the country to earn money and the world beats up on them.

The problem is it's almost impossible to get any capital together here. Per capita annual income is under two hundred dollars a year. Labor is unbelievably cheap, yet hordes remain unemployed. Even professional jobs like teaching pay less than three dollars a day. Indu, a science teacher at Byndabasini, age twenty-four, makes fifty dollars a month.

Indu's dream, and the dream of a large percentage of Nepali males, is to go to one of the industrialized countries: the United States, Japan, West Germany. Or if that's not possible, to one of the oil-rich countries that use foreigners to do their dirty-work: Kuwait before the war, Saudi Arabia, Brunei. There he thinks he could work for a few years, save some money, and return to Nepal. With this capital, the family would somehow escape the morass of poverty, or so he believes. Indu would buy a sewing machine, add another room to the house, put his daughter in the boarding school so she wouldn't be one of eighty in a classroom, and on and on. But Indu's chances of gaining employment in another country are very slim, unless he goes to India, which uses Nepalis as virtual slaves for factories, coal mines, and as night watchmen—or to Korea from where even grimmer stories emerge.

So Indu frets in a continual state of anxiety. He's educated to the point of awareness of what he doesn't have. And he wants it, as much for his children as for himself. But he can't get it. Scores and scores of young Nepali men disappear abroad, devoured by a system that discards them, or if they survive, they feel they can't return empty-handed, having left with all their family's hopes.

What Indu really wants, he confided, is to study computer science. Then he could get a job at a large business firm in Kathmandu. He's seen the advertisements in *The Rising Nepal*, the English newspaper. But to qualify for those jobs, he would have to study abroad. Maybe, he thinks, a man he once met at Lakeside will help him get a job in Germany. He's waiting for a letter....

I could tell several similar stories, and they make me sad. I don't blame the Nepalis for wanting some of the material things they've become aware of since the 1950s when the country was opened to the West. I certainly don't blame them for wanting to improve health and sanitation. But I don't like this restless gnawing that Indu exhibits, this feeling of inferiority about his own culture's accomplishments, and his deference to me. He thinks westerners must be smarter somehow because they are from a technologically advanced culture.

Nepal is not "behind" the West. It's just in a different place. And it has much that the West is crying for: stable families that guide children into a solid identification with their society as a whole, a spirituality that pervades their daily life, and a blend between work (that's still mostly honest physical labor) and play that validates the importance of enjoying life. We should be studying them to see how we can compensate for what we've lost before they've modernized so much that they have little left to teach.

5

Finally a mystery is solved. Lately, I've been hearing this "took, took, took" all day. I knew it was a bird, but I couldn't find it. Yesterday evening I was at my friend Clare Miller's for dinner. She teaches nursing at the medical campus in Pokhara. We were sitting on her back porch before we ate, watching two beautiful green birds with bright red patches on their chests and heads engaged in animated communication. When we identified them as crimson-breasted barbets, the book said that the call sounds like someone tapping on metal or the slow whistle of a rice mill, "took," repeated endlessly. Such a luxury I have here of worrying about small things.

For two hours yesterday afternoon the rain fell in an unrelenting deluge before it cleared. In that space of time I'm convinced the corn below my window grew at least a foot. Then the clouds to the north cleared off the mountains, and the sun did lovely things with reds and blues and silver shadows. New snow fell again on the Mardi Himal. While we sat on Clare's porch the birds quieted, but even when the sky darkened, we could see Machhapuchhare outlined like a faint pencil drawing, while to the south down the Pokhara valley, lightning still flashed.

This morning the mountains are positively brilliant. The brilliance won't last, of course, because a blue haze already steams over the valley. Right now the scene is almost too perfect to be real, like one of those murals on the walls of office complexes or official buildings. Even though I could outline all the ridges now from memory, I always go to the roof and pay homage.

I can see why foreigners stay here. Surely no place in the world is more beautiful. All the daily occurrences that seemed so strange and exotic at first seem natural now. I don't even notice them, or if I do, I wonder at my own prior amazement at something so normal. And even though the customs are so different, I have built my own island, taking in only that which comforts me and shutting out the rest. I do the same thing at home. I would no more think of attending the NFL games in America than I would the goat sacrifices of Dasaii here.

I suppose one can build that island anywhere. My friend Clare does that. Clare is in her sixties. She had a similar job in the Gambia before her teaching assignment here. When she finishes in Nepal, she wants to go to Jamaica for two years, possibly to stay. Her real commitment is to family planning and population control. She's been divorced for twenty years, but she has children—four, I think. At times she misses them. Her eyes were suddenly wet yesterday when she was telling me about the baby downstairs in her house. She had been present at the birth and said she couldn't help but feel how much her own daughters would have liked her with them at times like that. She has two grandchildren she's never seen.

I respect Clare. Of all the development work I've seen now, I say without reservation that her educational work in population control is the most important and positive contribution I have seen. Her concrete work in an area of need can actually affect the course of human development in a constructive way. How few times that can be said for all the billions of dollars spent on development. I salute her. She's not only doing her work, she's doing it well, with good humor and dignity.

But I'm not Clare, who carries her little island of home with her now and whose work is addressing an important problem for industrial and developing nations alike. My job seems of dubious need and merit. I'm not kidding myself anymore. But I am learning a lot about the importance of taking the time to listen to bird calls and to watch mountains draw pictures in the sky.

6

One of the hardest sights for me has been the public slaughter of the animals. The only safe species in Nepal are the cows. It's against the law to kill a cow. But goats, pigs, and water buffalo are butchered in full public view. I avoid the several days of ritual sacrifice. And cats and dogs lead dangerous lives indeed.

I've adjusted to conditions here I thought my antiseptic western mind would never tolerate. In fact, I've decided there is a virtue in honest visible dealings with harsh realities. No cellophane packages or cardboard buckets of Kentucky Fried Chicken hide the execution of poultry in Pokhara. If you want a chicken for dinner, you pick up a live one on your way home from work at the big basket pens in the market, drape it by the legs over your bike handlebars—I've never actually done this, having avoided all meat in Nepal—and wring its neck before plucking the feathers and throwing it in the pot. Or if you want *maasu*, meat, at your picnic, you take the live goat along; butchering it becomes part of the festivities. I've become inured to these practices, and I walk by meat stalls on my way to school barely averting my eyes from the severed heads. But the hanging of a dog left me weak and nauseated, and I had to go in my room and put my hands over my ears.

Dogs are a real and visible problem here. A veterinarian clinic exists in Pokhara, but getting a dog neutered is almost impossible for economic reasons. So the scores of cute little puppies turn into scrawny, unkept mutts that attach themselves to various households and become protective of scavenging rights. Rabies is still rampant and deadly.

Of course, ultimately, some method of control has to be

employed. I'm told that in Kathmandu on one day each year, the police scour the city and poison all the dogs they can find. I try to be rational about this. Thousands of dogs are "put to sleep" every day in the U.S. Each year I read an article in *The Oregonian* about the plight of unclaimed animals in Portland. I once took a stray to the Humane Society when I had been unable to find a home for it, knowing full well it had virtually no chance for adoption. It was an act which I have avoided thinking about ever since.

So when my housemate Shelby walked onto the porch and began screaming for me to come, I knew immediately it was something I didn't want to see and couldn't help. An awful melee filled the air: a high squealing from the dog itself swinging from a rope in the tree just across the little stream where the ducks gather, other dogs jumping and barking, and kids running to watch. I ran back in my room and covered my ears. My first impulse was to get my Swiss army knife and go to the rescue. I was surprised to find I had grabbed it. But even in my distress I knew what was happening. Chanda, downstairs, had said this was a *naraamro kakur*, a bad dog. They were getting rid of the dog deliberately.

Tragedies exist in painful evidence that I pass dry-eyed every day in Nepal. Each morning I see a beggar on the bridge with no legs and only one arm. Many children here are blind from preventable vitamin A deficiencies. I lay down on my mattress and held the pillow against my ears. I would not mourn the torturous death of a dog. Yet the image seared right through my eyelids and swung back and forth all day.

7

I am in a state of shock at a letter from my mother-in-law detailing a friend's death. She included several newspaper clippings. If I have the story at all straight, he was accused of some kind of involvement in child pornography, removed from his classroom by police, and later committed suicide. I am deeply shocked and grieved, both by the accusations and his death. I knew him as a compassionate, caring teacher and a sensitive person. My mind is grappling with this other information, which apparently has been so distorted by the press that the truth will be extremely hard to discover. I grieve for all whose lives have been damaged by this tragedy.

The newspaper accounts mentioned several times that he had spent two years in Thailand. The implication was that time spent in Thailand might explain interest in sexual practices considered aberrant by American society. I am not familiar with the sexual mores in Thailand. The sad scene in Bangkok is heavily patronized by western men, so that exploitation of young girls and boys is probably more a reflection of the West than it is of Thailand. But just last Saturday I had a conversation with a friend about sexual practices in Nepal that has me wondering what determines right and wrong in this business and who is qualified to judge.

I have little information about sexual customs in Nepal. I not only have been living a totally celibate life but have been enjoying the reprieve from the preoccupation with sex that commands one's more youthful years. But it doesn't take long to figure out that Nepal is fraught with the same kinds of contradictions that pervade other societies in their attitudes toward sex. Men and women do not touch each other in public. Girls and boys won't even sit on the same side of the classroom. While sex is supposedly reserved for marriage, even I have heard stories of illegal abortions and village prostitutes. And the sexuality of Shiva in his different manifestations is celebrated in various festivals.

My friend Joy is faced with a situation that would be clear-cut at home. She lives with a Tamang family. Among the family members who usually occupy the household is a twenty-two-year-old son and his wife. The wife has just had a baby and, as is the custom, has returned to her own mother for several weeks for an initiation into motherhood. The third night she was gone, Joy noticed that Bim, one of the boys from her sixth class, spent the night in the husband's room. The next night it happened again. The house is very small and it wasn't hard to figure out what was going on. She was alarmed, especially as she noticed that one of Bim's eyes looked a little funny, as if he'd been roughhousing. She asked him in class what was wrong with his eye. He just laughed, not embarrassed at all, and said he wasn't getting enough sleep these days. The other boys laughed as well. She decided to confront the situation head on. She went to the *aamaa*, the husband's mother, who was first in command in the house and seemed in other ways to run a most proper ship. Boldly, she asked why Bim was spending the night. The *aamaa* shrugged and smiled a little, a sort of boys-will-be-boys smile. Joy was stymied and confused. She felt quite sure that Bim was being sexually used. So she asked me what I thought she should do.

Now I would have said before that if there were one thing I was clear about in my mind concerning sex, it was that adults should not be using children sexually. In Oregon there are clear laws about such things, and a teacher in Joy's position would be legally bound to report this scene to the authorities. But neither Joy nor I are in Oregon. We are in a country where all the members of a family frequently sleep in the same room, sometimes even in the same bed. Whatever the prudishness in language (it is not even mentioned that a woman is pregnant), most Nepali children are exposed early to the realities of sex. In this society, displays of physical affection between males are frequent. Men walk down the street hand in hand. At my school, when there is a lack of chairs in the teachers' room, men freely sit on each other's laps. Whatever the ramifications of these unabashed displays of warmth, they are quite separate from the lifelong commitment to the economic unit of the marriage.

We talk about it, for this is a hard one. What will happen if Joy does nothing? In a few weeks, the wife will return, and Bim will be back out of the house. Is he damaged? Will he suffer the emotional trauma we associate with child victims of sexual abuse in the States? Probably not, we decide. He isn't embarrassed now, nor trying in any way to hide his behavior from others. If his society doesn't make him feel what was done was wrong, then he will not feel violated.

We both feel threatened. Surely we are not saying that our society is wrong, that it is all right for children to have sex. Suddenly I feel a little dizzy, like my mind is being stretched too close to the danger point. No, I'm not saying it is all right for children to have sex in our society, because they would suffer the consequences of having violated the rules, spoken or unspoken. But I can't speak for Nepal. I'm just a temporary worker here, and I tell Joy she should talk to our supervisor before she interferes in this situation. Right and wrong is much harder than it used to be.

Or maybe much easier. In Nepal, where cows are considered sacred because they lead souls to heaven, it is not morally acceptable to eat beef. Yet, my Nepali friend, Yogi, who was sent to a camp in California by an American environmental group, tried beef while he was there. He only stayed three months, but had he stayed longer, who knows, he might have adjusted to the custom that is regarded with horror here, and become a regular patron of McDonalds. When he returned to Nepal, he would have had to hide his acquired taste, even from his parents. They would have been mortified that their son flouted not only law and social custom, but holy writ as well.

Machhapuchhare at sunset

8

Sometime after the thunderstorm the sky became wondrously clear. Because the moon was full, the dogs barked all night. I woke to run at three-thirty. (I have to leave for school shortly past five.) I used my flashlight to put on my clothes because the electricity all over Pokhara went off with the storm. I slipped quietly through the iron gate.

I have run in the moonlight before, but never like this, with no competing lights from anywhere. The sky was flooded, blotting out the stars. In the north I could feel the snows on the mountains glowing, but I didn't look directly at them yet, because I wanted to save the sight for the moment when I turned the corner on the other road.

The first dogs I passed were hoarse from barking all night at the moon, but they roared at me anyway so I wouldn't forget their threat. Before I broke into a jog, I threaded my way through a donkey team grazing beside the road. The hair on their backs that had grown in white from sores reflected the light. They stood quietly and the bells tinkled on those that were feeding.

The road was clear and free from the jumping frogs that proliferate when it rains. I could hear the small Scopes owls in the tree by the nursing campus wall. The white trim on the row houses where the nurses live cut bold geometric lines. Another donkey team was scattered across the road. They stood silently, and the light was so bright I could see their sleepy, sideways ears.

The rocks that held down the roofs of the smaller houses made mottled patterns on the gleaming metal. At the intersection, which is noisy and cluttered with color during the day, were two cows, sleeping in silhouette in the middle of the road.

I turned left off the Kathmandu road, and at last I let myself look at the mountains. Someone had drawn them in fantastic and minute detail with chalk on black construction paper, carefully etching around each ridge and fold without a single smudge. Then the drawing had been hung in soft illumination against a blue-black drape. Machhapuchhare neatly rose to a point in the center, with the wide snowfields of the Annapurnas sloping in sharply defined curves.

Then the mosque on the left side of the road came into focus. This little mosque, which in the daylight seems a small and forlorn misfit, now captured all the dignity of its heritage. Its white walls gleamed cleanly, and the slender minarets pointed boldly upward, like the sacred Machhapuchhare, toward the god. Each tower was intersected by black bands that made the whole structure seem magically suspended. From the interior, which glowed like old bronze, came a chanting murmur.

I ran to where the road narrowed and turned between the little shops. A large orange house, so imposing in the daylight with its carved windowsills, was a dark shape. Now it was distinguished from the rest of the buildings only by its hulk. I ran a little faster. The curved white dome of the small Shiva *mandir* by the road shone softly.

I had not seen a single person. As I slowed to walk the gravel lane to my house, the moon seemed to blink. The sky had just broken a blue line in the east.

9

It's May! And my school is closed for elections. The rumor kept circulating that we would close, but no schedule for the closure was announced in advance. Finally the headsir told us that we would close next week. But once a vacation is in the air here, it magically expands. Today is only Wednesday and we're shut down already.

I have exciting news. I'm going over to Solu Khumbu, the Everest area in eastern Nepal famed for its Sherpa culture, with Dorothy Mierow. Dorothy has been in Nepal twenty-seven years and has established a natural history museum in Pokhara. Clare and I visited Dorothy's museum yesterday for the first time. It is a positive delight, full of paintings or bas-relief of flowers, birds, plants, and butterflies and free-standing sculptures of animals. Dorothy is an artist and has done most of the work herself. The only real animal is a stuffed leopard. Dorothy told a story of having watched the men of Pokhara stone the leopard to death after chasing it and trapping it against a cliff. She took us out back and pointed out the exact area by the river. The leopard had mauled three women. After the men killed it, they all wanted a souvenir. Dorothy persuaded them to give it to the museum while it was only missing a few teeth, some whiskers, and the end of its tail.

Dorothy said that a child was killed by a leopard in Pokhara last year. He probably was outside relieving himself, as she delicately put it. The leopards come into Pokhara at night, she said, pointing out some hillside caves where they are known to live, and kill street dogs for food. And I've been running out there in the dark.

Clare and I were sitting in Dorothy's office while she was

finishing another mural panel of animals, which was stretched along the wall. I told Dorothy I was thinking of going over to Solu Khumbu and impulsively asked her if she would like to come. She looked at me thoughtfully for a few seconds, and said yes, she'd love to. She needed to go into Kathmandu and make her arrangements for returning to Colorado this summer anyway. She would love a chance to trek in the east again and see what changes had taken place there. So not only am I going to see Mt. Everest, I'm going with my very own natural history expert. She has written several books on botany and wildlife in Nepal. Dorothy must be seventy, but she'll probably hike me into the ground. We'll leave Saturday morning. I said my only requirement for this trip was to see a yak, so she promised me I would.

A large section in Dorothy's museum houses a magnificent collection for Colin Smith, a foremost authority on Himalayan butterflies. Colin came here from London twenty-five years ago. He was in the back room working on photographs for a new atlas of Nepal's butterflies when Clare and I walked into the display area. When he saw us, he came out with a little flutter and settled beside us like a kindly, fragile grey moth with slightly ragged wings. He ushered us through several specimen drawers of incredibly delicate artistic miniatures with beautiful names like snow Apollo, Krishna peacock, and treble silverstripe—not to be confused, he said, with a small silverfork. When he showed us something particularly delightful, he bounced up on his toes as if he were hopping to the next flower. (I was so fascinated I found myself rising unconsciously in rhythm with him.) He wore a soft grey shirt with small butterflies embroidered where there had been pockets and another big butterfly in the center of his back. Then suddenly, right in the middle of a discourse, he floated off, and when I looked up from the drawer, he was back in the glassed-in workroom bending over the photographs again.

What a delightful man, I said to Clare on our way out. What a delightful way to spend your life, cataloging all these miniature works of natural beauty that pass most of us unnoticed. She was not nearly as impressed and proceeded to describe in detail a mystery story she'd just finished in which the protagonist had been a collector of butterflies and then started collecting beautiful women the same way. I was the one who had been so upset over the war, she insisted. How could I be so forgiving of a man who suffocated butterflies? She had a point.

All those butterflies had lost their brief chance in the sun. But while he talked, Colin had mourned the destruction of trees that ruined the habitat for butterflies and mentioned sightings in remote areas that most people will never reach. I could not think of this strange, gentle man as a killer of butterflies. He seemed a priest, who shares secrets with the rest of us who haven't reached his enlightened state. His sacrifices open doors of beauty to the inner mystery that, understood and shared together, might someday save us all.

Woman spinning wool at the Tibetan refugee camp

10

Dorothy and I do not leave Pokhara for Solu Khumbu until tomorrow on the early mail bus, so I've had another day to play without feeling responsible to any schoolwork. I went with Clare to the Tibetan refugee camp west of Pokhara to visit the carpet factory. Clare had never been there before and was delighted. This is not a story about the despair of exploited workers. This small factory is airy and well ventilated. The women sing and laugh at the looms and comb each other's hair. The rugs they make are beautiful.

A new temple has just opened in the camp, built with donated money. All refugee camps should have such a picturesque setting, with Himalayas in the background and long-haired sheep with curly horns. A dormitory for the monks stands behind the temple. I am endeared to the youngest monks-in-training. Much reverence is attached to them, especially if they are considered a reincarnation of an important lama, such as one who was pointed out to us by an older monk today. The boy, about seven or eight, was playing with a toy car.

I was still thinking about that little boy when I climbed to my roof for the nightly drama I've come to expect since the pre-monsoon showers began this spring. The evening clouds promised to be spectacular, as today's thunderstorm got muddled and just grumbled around without much rain. I liked the idea of finding some part of god in a little child playing with toys. When I stepped out on the roof, the sun suddenly re-emerged, low in the west. If ever I saw a childhood picture of the Judeo-Christian heaven, this was it. To the east behind the Buddhist monastery hill, several layers of clouds were stacked, moving in different directions and speeds in the wind. The lowest layer of grey-blue slate-like clouds flowed northward. Above that a boiling layer of orange streamed the other way. A stationary band of pink fluff just sat on top of all the other activity. Above the pink fluff, majestic white thunderheads arched and puffed in huge cornices against the bluest sky. In front of all this stood the little orange temple with its shimmering golden roof, surely the house where god lives. From it resonated an awful squawking of horns and gongs like noisy angels practicing.

The house where god lives, monastery in Pokhara

VIII

TREKKING TO TENGBOCHE WITH DOROTHY AND THE LAMA

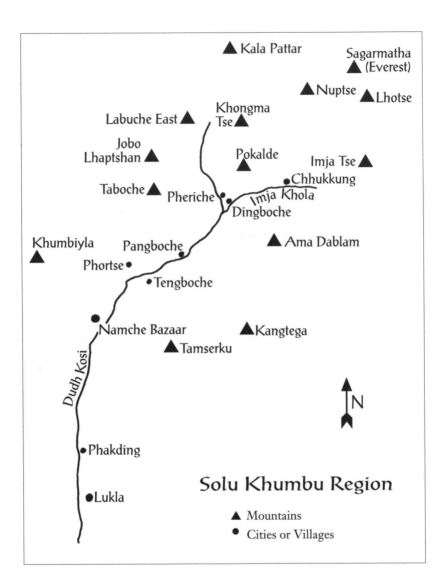

Solu Khumbu Region

▲ Mountains
● Cities or Villages

▲

May 6

The flight to Lukla set the stage for the beauty and romance that would accompany me for this entire trip. I felt as if I were on the back of one of the Himalayan griffons that had soared above us on the climb to the Mardi Himal. The small plane skimmed in and out of clouds over the green mountains with the huge himals off to the left. We landed on the small upward-sloping grass and gravel airstrip, already at 9,500 feet elevation.

Our flight was met by four Sherpas looking for work as guides and porters. We chose the oldest, a short man of extremely slight build, who looked as if he needed work and would be willing to go slowly when we stopped to look for birds. He asked politely if he could go to his house to pick up his coat and a few provisions, so we followed him past the Hillary school, circling a cluster of grey-white *chortens*, Buddhist shrines, crowned with prayer flags.

The house was a very traditional Sherpa dwelling. The downstairs, which belonged to the animals, was occupied only by a small black and white dog with three very new puppies. She growled softly at our intrusion but did not leave the nest of straw. A steep wooden ladder led from the semi-darkness to the family level. I felt I had climbed into the center of a hollow tree where sunshine filtered through the cracks. The room was all soft natural browns and golds.

The floor of smooth wooden planks was swept clean. Five small children were gathered in the kitchen area, eating a thick soup. One, dressed in blue wool and blue boots, lifted a white bowl to his lips. The spacious and tidy room contained sleeping rugs and mats rolled and stacked on the closed trunks. A chimneyless fire, built on a raised platform and fed with wood, smoldered. A collection of large pots, kettles, and plates was displayed on one wall. The copper, bronze, and brass were so highly polished that the side of the room radiated a soft burnished glow. Oblong tin storage boxes and cupboards of dark wood lined another wall. The ceiling, hand-hewn cedar planks, was darkened by the smoke. Two large wooden prayer wheels, colorful cylinders at least five feet high with prayers carved in large Tibetan letters, stood in front of each of the windows.

The man motioned us to open a narrow door at the end of the room. Through the doorway we saw an arrangement of books and white statues of the Buddha. The shrine seemed more elaborate than the usual household sanctuary. "Why, I think he's a lama," said Dorothy, and she asked him. Sure enough, he nodded in assent. The term is used rather loosely, and Dorothy surmised that he was of the lay preacher variety, perhaps responsible for certain religious duties within the community. Immediately before we left he performed a special ceremony, burning juniper leaves in the smoldering fire to insure good fortune on our journey.

We walked for three hours on a gradual slope up the cleft of the valley. The tiny fairy gentians and primula bloomed on the sides of the hill. Silver green leaves and delicate flowers of the beam trees, *sorbus cuspidata*, shimmered in the bright sun. Among the slender yellow jasmine we saw a large swallow-tailed butterfly. While we walked we heard the monotonous call of the large hawk cuckoo and the song, a long dominate note, of the black-capped sibia. Dorothy told me to watch for a bright brick-orange bird.

We stopped for the day before two o'clock at Phakding, before the long ascent to Namche Bazaar. The lama, after he was assured we were settled for the day, asked if he could return to his family for the night. We gave our approval and he set off briskly.

After eating lunch, we took our binoculars and climbed a little hill off the main trail. We sat down in some trees with a view of the stream below that tumbled among the boulders. A warbler song teased us, but the first bird we got a good look at was the gray-backed shrike, a lovely large shrike with a golden breast, black mask around the eyes, and blue-grey back. Then a male white-capped river chat put on quite a show. He first posed conveniently against a grey backdrop of a boulder, a pretty, colorful bird with a large white patch on the top of his head, a black front half of

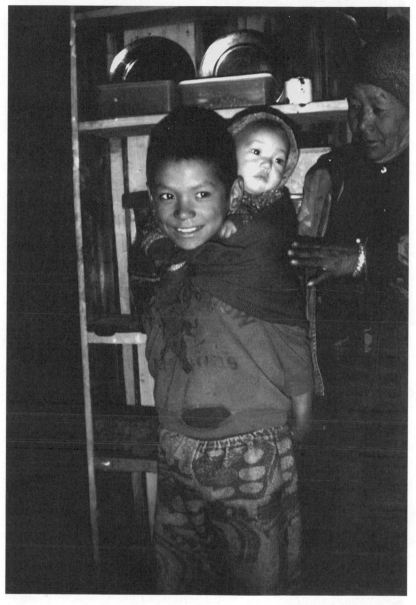

Sherpa children at home in Lukla

the body but bright red back. He played in the water like a dipper and continually wagged his bright red tail.

Next we saw a green-backed tit, yellow, green, and black with a white cheek patch. We could see the warblers, but they were flitting around so fast that I couldn't fasten the glasses on them. We moved up the hill a bit and sat down under a tree in the grass. Soon they came closer, and Dorothy identified two species, the Tickell's leaf warbler and the yellow-eyed warbler. On the way back to the lodge we saw a pair of brown birds that turned out to be plain-colored laughing thrushes.

Later we sat under a small solar-battery-powered light and ate our dinner. My favorite photograph of all, I said, in your *Himalayan Flowers and Trees*, is the one of the jack-in-the-pulpits and the morel mushrooms. She said she had taken that picture on the trail from Chitre to Gandruck in the days when there was hardly any trail at all, in the late 1960s or early 70s. The picture was taken close to where she found an American boy who was hiding from the Vietnam War. His visa had run out as had his passport. He was a Buddhist who had taken a vow of silence and he wrote all this on a piece of slate.

He had no money and practically no food. She had the porters show him how to make nettle soup by picking the nettles between sticks and boiling them. (They'd made some for her earlier and she thought it was quite delicious, although a little slimy.) She also gave him a letter to show to the principal at her college in Pokhara, asking that he be given a job to earn money for bus fare to Kathmandu.

She didn't see him for three years. Then one day she was in Kathmandu and had gone with friends to the monastery close to the cave where Milarepa spent years meditating in silence. (Milarepa was a Newari Buddhist who is much revered for his beautiful poetry.) A special service was being held for monks who had observed three years of silence. They were coming out of their caves and could talk again. Who should be among them but this American man, who had been in his cave for three years. When he saw her he said, "Why, Dorothy, I was just thinking about you." His visa and passport had been amended through influential intervention from America and he could legally stay in Nepal.

She went back to see the young man a couple of times, taking cauliflower, which was a luxury vegetable in Kathmandu, and once he served her with cake that he had baked. After that she lost touch with him for a few years until she went to Copan, a meditative center out toward Bodnath. There he was again. He was passing out *prasad*, the food which is offered to and accepted by the god and then shared with the worshippers. That was the last time she saw him.

The air was cold in the lodge but we sat at the table for an hour bundled in our coats. Dorothy read aloud from the Dalai Lama book I had brought along. We went to bed early so as not to waste the lodge's battery for the light.

▲

May 7

The lama had returned by six-thirty when we awoke. We started from Phakding at seven and right away the birding was spectacular. The plain-colored laughing thrush was in the bushes by the lodge again, and as we started across the bridge we saw the white-capped river chat. Dorothy recognized the whistling thrush, a plain bird with a beautiful song. Before we were a hundred yards from the bridge, we'd seen a slender black and white pied wagtail and a yellow-headed wagtail as well. But what we kept hearing was the black-capped sibia that had eluded us yesterday. The trail led steeply from the bridge and at a curve where it leveled, Dorothy sat down. Right on cue a large brick-orange bird with a black-crested cap perched in the tree in front of her and sang its song.

There were hundreds of yellow flowers, Himalayan euphorbia. We were in a deep gorge of the Dudh (milk) Kosi and the river was milky grey. We met *chaumri*, which our lama called zup-yuks, a mix between yaks and cows, with red tassels in their ears. They are important pack animals and wear bells that clang musically as they walk. We entered the Sagarmatha National Park. At the entry station was a reproduction of a bird chart that Dorothy had painted several years ago for the schoolchildren of Nepal.

The leaf warbler sang incessantly as we hiked along the trail. For a brief time we saw the snowfields and rippling crevasses of Tamserku up the valley, but soon it was hidden behind other ridges. At a waterfall we saw a plumbeous redstart, a slate-blue male with a maroon tail that bobbed continually. Our lama made sure we stayed to the left of all the *mani* stones. *Mani* stones are carved with Tibetan prayers. We felt it important to show respect.

We talked about the Dalai Lama's teachings that Dorothy had read aloud the night before. We were both impressed at the holy man's attitude toward other religions. He defines the common objectives as love, respect, and alleviation of suffering. His words regarding Christianity reflect tolerance and reverence. Dorothy said the Christians who had first come to Nepal did not have this attitude toward Buddhism and Hinduism, which is why laws exist against proselytizing. An outsider who has converted a Nepali to another religion faces a prison sentence, as does the Nepali convert.

When Dorothy first came to Pokhara, she used to have dinner with the Shining Hospital missionary crowd. They didn't ask her about the state of her soul, for they assumed she was saved. But when the general director came from the Congo, his wife was suspicious of Dorothy's religious convictions and followed her home. The wife pointed out to Dorothy that she was in a primary position to subtly influence souls to be saved. Dorothy said she hadn't read enough about Hinduism and Buddhism to know whether those souls needed saving from anything. The director's wife was taken aback and counseled Dorothy not to read anything but the Bible to avoid falling victim to doubts.

We stopped for lunch early. The lama said it was a long way before we could buy food again. The air was cool in the little tea shop, so I sat outside on a wooden bench where I could see the river. A whistling thrush flew in a long, slanted line from a tree by the river to an apple tree against a house and continued the song there. Ubiquitous cabbage butterflies, white with a few black spots, floated among the potato and mustard plants. A pink rhododendron in full bloom leaned from the cliff above the water.

For a long time we hiked among the boulders, then began the stiff uphill trail. We crossed the Dudh Kosi on a high suspension

Dorothy Mierow and friends

bridge where it joined the Bhote Kosi, which flows from Tibet. We saw the first tiny purple iris with delicate variegated petals. Waterfalls tumbled through slanted patches of snow on the other side of the gorge. Dorothy felt the altitude but rested often and never complained. I was whistling "Ash Grove," and when we stopped hiking, she joined with a lovely harmony. A little farther on she sang a little song with a fragile yodel, so I told her about my uncle's coming across the field in the morning, yodeling, and all the barn cats hearing the song and lining up on the top fence board, waiting to be fed.

A damp slope that turned into a stream harbored much bird activity, but we couldn't see well through the leafy bushes. Dorothy sat down to rest. Then, as if on command for her, the female of the white-winged grosbeak with its golden underside hopped out from under a bush and fed quietly in full view. We passed more iris, and a boy drove a flock of long-haired sheep past us. One had horns so curled they encircled its ears. There were a few shaggy lambs who scrambled past with infant cries.

The mountain laburnum, a yellow bush that looks like Scotch broom, covered the hillside as we topped out at Namche Bazaar. The clouds boiled over the highest peaks. The late afternoon sun no longer gave warmth as we entered the amphitheater of the colorful little town.

▲

May 8

Rosy finches chattered in the bushes as we began the steep hill up from Namche Bazaar. Snow-covered peaks surround the little town, which is filled with colorful lodges and long-haired yaks. Namche is a central meeting point for many expeditions and climbs. We had considered staying another day, but Dorothy felt more rested in the morning and was poring over the map when I woke.

Dorothy had stayed in Namche for a couple of months several years ago, working in the museum on the hill, painting charts of trees for the National Parks and UNICEF. She pointed out the little house with a prayer flag and tree in the yard where she had lived. Twice a day she had hiked up and down the trail that

*Temple with eyes that search for the good in the world,
in the village of Kundi, Solu Khumbu*

climbed a thousand feet to the museum. Her paintings are still part of the exhibits. I pulled my copy of *Himalayan Flowers and Trees* from my pack and showed it to the lama. He stopped and took the book in his hands, turning the pages carefully. He understood that Dorothy was the author and he saluted her respectfully. She smiled graciously in return.

As we crested the ridge for a full view of the glaciers on Tamserku, we saw the first lammergeier. It circled quite close and we could see the wide wing span (up to nine feet, the largest bird in Nepal) and the orange head and underside. These enormous birds, almost extinct in northern Europe, are used for disposal of the dead at the highest altitudes, where fuel is scarce for cremation and the soil is rocky. The body is prepared and "given to the birds."

Small skipper butterflies, brown with wings held back at rest, sat on the path. Full slopes shimmered with purple iris, and we saw the first blooms of "black" pea, which are close to the ground and not black at all, but bluish purple. A white-rumped swift darted above us. "The fastest bird in the world," said Dorothy. Swifts have been clocked in India flying from cliff to cliff at speeds of over a hundred miles an hour.

Then we rounded the ridge for the first view of Everest. The tip slanted to the left behind the long line of the Lhotse-Nuptse ridge with Ama Dablam's strange horned pyramid hulk to the right. On a high saddle we could see the Tengboche monastery's roof shining. I felt there should have been an orchestrated symphonic crescendo, but only the resonant musical clanging of a yak bell sounded. The lammergeier circled against the sun.

Suddenly to the left we spotted a small herd of Himalayan thar, the brown mountain goat, halfway up the slope. We were both excited, but Dorothy was especially pleased. She knew they had become scarce. Perhaps they were making a comeback due to the protection of the national park. I climbed up for pictures and got quite close before they moved aside. When I returned to the path, we decided the photos would be better with Dorothy's camera so I started back up. After a few steps, I realized Dorothy was behind me. This was the closest she had ever been, she said excitedly, so we went up together, moving quietly. The lovely little herd of eight with three young were a reddish-brown fawn color with short slanted horns and graceful necks. The padded rumps showed their relation to the antelope family. They posed nicely on the rocks before moving quietly to the left after a pica's shrill whistle. We congratulated each other like schoolgirls.

Ama Dablam came more fully into view. Large glaciers hung improbably suspended on its pointed peak. "There's the locket," Dorothy said. Ama Dablam means mother's locket.

Then we saw a second herd of Himalayan thar. This time a shaggy long-haired male stretched out in the sun on a wide rock. I decided to climb up again, they were so beautiful. I took both cameras. As I started, a flock of snow pigeons banked against the hill above them. To the west was the white of the old moon. I climbed very close to a mother and her kid. They eyed me nervously, then moved over with the rest of the herd. I waited for the large male to get up, but he simply watched quietly across the deep gully between us. I came down awkwardly. The goats moved away easily and gracefully.

Rounding the corner, we were suddenly in the midst of white and pink rhododendrons in full bloom. We took pictures of Ama Dablam framed in blossoms and then emerged to a park-like meadow. Here Dorothy once met the Flemings, who wrote the authoritative *Birds of Nepal*, camped with a group of birders. We stopped for a bowl of soup at the *chiyaa* shop.

The rhododendrons clustered in large bushes full of colorful blooms. Yellow catkins and budding leaves hung on the birches. Several years ago Dorothy had come through here in March with a friend. They had a lovely surprise at Tengboche when it stormed during the night. They woke up to yaks covered with a thick blanket of snow.

As we waited for our soup, we drank tea and I asked Dorothy about her life. She told me of her childhood in Colorado, the tragic death by drowning of an older sister, the years of care for a mother severely crippled by a stroke, and her special closeness to her father, who was a professor of classics. She traveled extensively around the world with him before his death. She came to Nepal when her father died, and has been here much of the time since. Before that she taught geography at Colorado College and was curator of the natural history museum there. She was forty when she came to Nepal in 1962. Since then she has taught school, built a museum in Pokhara, and written several books on the natural history of Nepal.

When we resumed trekking, the trail slanted in a long, slow line from the level meadow. Scores of yellow butterflies ascended, like flakes of sunshine. We stopped and watched. "Just the common yellow sulfur," Dorothy said. The butterflies had touched a memory for her. "Do school children still memorize poetry and give long recitations?" she asked. "Hardly," I laughed, thinking of my struggles to get students to memorize lines from Shakespeare. Well, whenever she saw a big batch of yellow butterflies she thought of those long recitation programs she remembered from her childhood. Each year someone recited a long, sad poem about a mother who had lost her son in war. The poem started with a little boy running in the sun with a flock of yellow butterflies around his hair. But he disappeared in the war and the mother searched and searched for him. Finally she went to Arlington cemetery, and when she reached the tomb of the unknown soldier a host of yellow butterflies rose from it, and she knew it was her son. And here we were in Nepal, seeing the same butterflies. "Are they all over the world?" I asked, for her sentimental story had made me sad. "Oh yes, it's the common yellow sulfur. They're all over the world."

Looking back on the ridge behind us over the terraced potato fields, Dorothy pointed out the area of the luxury Everest View Hotel. The developers had wanted to put the airstrip in the potato fields, but were persuaded by the Sherpas to use the other side. Every patch of land that can be cultivated at this altitude is precious.

Our path was leading up to a pass in the ridge. We had parted with the wider trail to Tengboche and were headed for Phortse. The wind increased as we rose above the rhododendrons. The yellow-billed chouch, the bird that flies the highest, glided low over the grass. Yaks grazed above us on the hillside. Even when we couldn't see them, we could hear their bells.

Finally we reached the *chorten*, shrine, at the pass. The jagged peaks of Tamserku were visible through windows in the clouds. Beside the *chorten* was a cluster of *mani* stones. Prayer flags whipped wildly in the cold wind. Dust swirled in tight circles.

The tea shop where we took refuge from the wind was filled with smoke because there was no chimney for the stove. As we drank the smoky-tasting tea, a black and white cow-yak put a friendly face in the doorway and looked at us curiously.

We left the warmth of the tea shop. The trail dropped precipitously into a narrow, deep gorge with magnificent rapids, waterfalls, and sculptured palisades. As we leveled at the river, we saw a winter wren and a coal tit with a tufted head. We crossed the river on a bridge of planks and stones, and we sat for a minute on the other side. A pair of white-winged grosbeaks settled in a tree. The male was larger and brighter green and yellow than the female.

As the trail rose again from the river, we met three magnificently shaggy yaks, just at the spot where we saw the first lavender rhododendrons. Large birch trees with peeled amber bark and drooping lichens hung over us. In western Nepal birch bark is still used for paper.

We topped the ridge at another *chorten*, this one surrounded with a long oblong wall of *mani* stones. Next to the wall stood a majestic golden yak, with a saddle and large bell. We entered the village of Phortse. The sparse separate houses had a lonely look about them and the wind whipped the dirt in our faces. A shaggy black yak was pulling a one-point plow. One man led the yak. Another followed, standing on the plow as it dug into rough spots. A woman walked behind, scattering the seeds of millet or buckwheat. A large black dog, a Tibetan mastiff, lunged at his chain as we passed.

Dorothy and I were given a room in a shed with a dirt floor partially covered with a yak hide. We ate our dinner of boiled potatoes in the main house with the family. The owner of the lodge was a Sherpa who had been on nineteen climbing expeditions. He spoke English fairly well and told us the villagers of Phortse were worried about their school. The school was one of

the much-touted Hillary schools established by the famous mountaineer. It was designed to serve the five primary classes. Because
of the harsh living conditions, teachers did not want to be assigned
to the village, so much of the time the school was closed. When
the older children were sent down to Khumjung for further schooling, they were teased for their poverty. The Sherpa's two daughters
sat on his lap and an old woman hunched by the fire, twirling a
prayer wheel and murmuring. Dorothy and I went to bed early
because of the cold.

▲

May 9

During the night we heard rain on the tin roof of the shed where
we slept under a blanket of yak wool. When Dorothy entered the
main house to see about breakfast, the Sherpa and his family were
still snuggled together under blankets, all in one bed in the kitchen
area.

High to the northwest above Phortse rose Khumbiyla, a mountain sacred to the Sherpas, the lama reverently informed us. A
flock of snow pigeons banked against it as we started. A blue-
fronted redstart sat on the wall above the field where the men
were already ploughing with the yak. We climbed the steep slope
to fine views of Tamserku's glaciers, and as I walked ahead, I could
see a lammergeier circling against the sheer rock face of the sacred mountain. I wondered if any bodies had been given to the
bird that day.

I gave Dorothy some water, then I hiked faster, feeling a little
disloyal. The clouds were moving up the lower valleys, and I wanted
good clear views to the east. The top of Ama Dablam showed
around the ridge. I hurried ahead, then stopped. Ama Dablam
had come into full view with its strange, flat pyramid top. To the
left was the Lhotse-Nuptse ridge. On a ribbed ridge of the immediate left skyline, a shaggy Himalayan thar stood in silhouette.
I sat down on a rock and waited for Dorothy and the lama.

The trail started to climb steeply. We came closer to the thar
that was now feeding on the tufts of grass on the vertical side of
the cliff. He was large and beautiful with thick horns and his long

Yak and chorten *at Phortse,*
Solu Khumbu

hair rippled in the wind. We continued to climb. We must have been over 14,000 feet as we looked down on Tengboche and the rhododendron blooms. Dorothy was disappointed we hadn't seen an Impeyan pheasant in such prime habitat. Another lammergeier circled and a large butterfly, yellow and black with distinctive rows of red and blue spots, landed for display right in front of us. We could see the buildings of a Buddhist nunnery below us.

The lama seldom spoke unless we asked direct questions. He knew only a few words of English and was obviously less comfortable with Nepali than the Sherpa language, which neither Dorothy nor I could speak. But he helped us watch for birds and animals. He treated us both with respect, but with Dorothy he was positively reverential. He cut a sturdy walking stick for her and insisted on carrying everything, even her camera. Twice he asked me her age and shook his head in wonder.

The wind was cold and gusty, so despite the good views of Everest, we were anxious to move on. We were tired and hungry. The trail dropped to the village of Pangboche. We saw the colorful male of the white-winged grosbeak by a little stream. The clouds swarmed around the high peaks, and we decided to stop at a lodge run by monks from the Pangboche monastery. The monks heated water in a pail and we took it to the shower house. We spent a pleasant afternoon getting clean.

Toward evening we walked through the village to the monastery that is purported to be the oldest in the region. Although the building was small and shabby, it housed some of the magnificent painted masks that are used in the Mani-Rimdu dances, a twice-yearly festival that celebrates the victory of the Buddha over the older Bon religion. Gracing the walls were elaborately carved wooden statues, some of the male and female deities in embrace. The lama lit oil lamps for us. This monastery for years gained a little extra income by exhibiting *yeti*, abominable snowman, relics, but the lama told us mournfully they had been stolen a few months earlier by trekkers who broke into the monastery at night.

Back in the lodge I asked the lama and Dorothy for *yeti* stories. Dorothy said there were various species of *yetis*. The most evil were the women, who were very beautiful but had their feet on backwards. Men, however, were usually so taken by the female *yetis'* beauty that this anatomical aberration was not noticed until the men had been lured away from their homes and then it was too late. All that was ever found of them were the bones.

Male *yetis* were of a more honest type, Dorothy said, and usually ate only yaks. She told one odd story of a doctor on an expedition, however, who was lured away by a male *yeti*. He was taken to treat a female *yeti* who had something stuck in her throat. He removed the object and then was taken back to the expedition. When he examined the object later, it turned out to be a human bone.

The lama told us about the Pangboche *yeti*. He was a benign type of *yeti*, who made friends with a very kindly monk. For many years he lived in a cave by the monastery and helped the monk with his work. When the *yeti* died, the monk preserved the skull cap and the hand, and those relics are what had been on display until a few months ago. Dorothy added later that this skull was once taken to the Smithsonian for analysis. Smithsonian scientists decided the skull was that of an animal, perhaps a Himalayan thar, stretched over human bone.

I asked Dorothy how seriously she took the *yeti* stories. Expeditions have searched for the *yeti* and unexpected people give it credence. Some people certainly believe something is out there, she said, and a few years ago she'd read a story in the paper about a *Sherpani*, Sherpa woman, who saw a *yeti* kill three yaks. The *Sherpani* was practically incoherent after the experience. In Dorothy's opinion, the creature in question (something was obviously behind all the sightings) was a bear. The brown bear lives above the tree line, is seldom sighted, and would be quite capable of killing yaks. But if Dorothy were trying to fund an expedition, scientific or otherwise, she'd be willing to add a *yeti* or two to her research because that attracted attention and money.

We slept well. When I went outside during the night, I saw no evidence of *yetis* at all, just billions of stars and the black hulk of Ama Dablam looming over the monastery.

*Tengboche monastery
in the shadow of Ama Dablam*

▲

May 10

A thin layer of ice topped the water in the bucket outside the door in the morning. Dorothy had decided to revise her plan of the night before. She had thought she would rest for a day and have me go to the village of Pheriche with the lama for a day hike. But in the morning she said she wanted to see for herself how Pheriche had changed. The last time she was there the settlement was only a temporary summer shelter for yak herders, with three huts. She and her friends had slept in the yak shelter, warmed by a fire of yak dung. It smoked so much they went outside for a while, but it was so cold they had to come back in. She was somewhat apologetic. Would I be disappointed not to have at least one day to go fast? No, I assured her. We had already seen far more than I had anticipated. I didn't mind going slowly, I said, and I meant it.

The trail rose in a series of steps. When we stopped at a stream, a blue-fronted redstart, with its steel-blue head and neck and rosy orange underside, perched in a tree just up the hill. Snow pigeons floated over a place where the river was somewhat dammed from an earlier landslide.

Rounding the corner, we could see the top of Everest again. We stopped by another stream where pussy willows were budding. A white-capped river chat bobbed its red tail, and a raven flew over to inspect Dorothy's cookie.

As the trail began to climb, the dryness increased. The ridge to the southwest of Tamserku and Kangtega was an incredible panorama of peaks. The shape of Ama Dablam had changed to two pyramids with the forward face showing a cavernous overhang. In front of the Lhotse-Nuptse ridge were huge brown moraines slanting in gravelly triangles. The black lava peaks of Pokalde reached up in gnarled and knotted fingers.

At the crest of the ridge, I stopped to wait for Dorothy and the lama. From the top of a small *chorten*, which was almost smothered in *mani* stones, a bleached prayer flag, its prayers scattered, whipped frantically. I sat down in the shelter of a large *mani* stone. I could see the snowfields stretching behind the first line of peaks.

Five women carrying large blue barrels with tumplines came up the trail from Pheriche, probably on their way to Namche Bazaar to purchase supplies.

We dropped down the ridge into Pheriche. No longer was it merely the yak huts of Dorothy's earlier visit. We saw a cluster of houses, trekker inns, and a mountaineering medical center which kept a special bag into which a person suffering from altitude sickness could be placed. The bag would be filled with air until the pressure was that of 8,000 feet. The doctor, an American woman, assured us there was ample business for the bag, because many people did not take adequate time to adjust to altitude.

Pheriche, a cold and windy place, afforded spectacular mountain views. To the west was the sliced-off face and snowcap of Taboche, and a little to the north of it a ruffled ridge of snow defined the top of JoBo Lhaptshan. Toes of two glaciers snaked down out of a cluster of peaks crowned by Labuche East. The black ridge of Pokalde hid Lhotse-Nuptse, but Ama Dablam stood in two separate pyramid peaks, the forward flaked like a colossal arrowhead, worked to perfection by a giant hand.

Dorothy felt rested after lunch and decided we should continue to Dingboche. I climbed over a ridge to a *chorten* while Dorothy and the lama circled on a lower trail. The landscape was bleak and beautiful. We reached Dingboche about three o'clock.

A Sherpa who was an experienced mountain climber operated the lodge in which we stayed. We heard from him of the Sherpa expedition that had summited Everest a few days before. The summit party was composed of three Sherpas and an American photographer. This expedition was an important milestone for Nepali pride. The Sherpas, one of the ethnic groups of the Solu Khumbu region, have been so important in the history of westerners' Himalayan conquests that their very name evokes romance for mountain climbers. Yet, in reality, the Sherpa men have been much abused by foreign climbing expeditions. Many have been killed helping foreigners achieve glory.

That evening as we sat by the warm yak-dung fire, Dorothy and I talked of mountain climbing. I told her how I had met Jim climbing Mount St. Helens and how we'd built a bond with

Sundeki, the didi *at the Sonam Friendship Lodge, Dingboche*

mountains as the thread. She told me of the other mountain climbers she knew, and they were prestigious indeed.

One was Sir Edmund Hillary, himself, who has a tragic tie with Dorothy. Dorothy's closest friend Barbara was killed in a plane crash with Hillary's wife and daughter and the Hillary dogs. Barbara had married a Sherpa whose family donated land to Hillary for a hospital in Phaflu. She and her husband were going with the Hillarys to inspect the progress of the hospital. The plane, which was hurriedly moved off the runway and into the air because the king was coming, crashed near Bodnath monastery in Kathmandu and killed them all.

Another famous mountaineer Dorothy knew was Willie Unsoeld of the first American Everest Expedition. He was in development work in Kathmandu during the sixties and was Dorothy's supervisor. She spent many hours with the family and was with his wife, Jolene Unsoeld, when Willie reached the top of Everest with the first American expedition. Dorothy also knew his daughter Devi well, both as a child and as a young adult working in Kathmandu the summer before the ill-fated expedition during which Devi died on her namesake mountain.

I dreamed that night about being home, and I woke up feeling incredibly lonesome for Jim. I lay awake a long time thinking about him and feeling a little bit wrong about seeing all this mountain beauty without him.

▲

May 11

We heard a thunderstorm during the night, and in the morning the ground around the lodge was covered with snow. We decided to spend another night at Dingboche and hike up to Chhukhung, the highest settlement in this glacial valley. As we started, the sky was alive with flashes of rosy finches and the golden breasts of blue-fronted redstarts. The wind was already whipping the snow in high spirals off the Lhotse-Nuptse ridge.

As we ascended the valley, snow and ice surrounded us. A long gleaming glacier loomed on the right. Behind us Taboche Peak's glacier tumbled down the sheer face like a waterfall. A band of yellow sandstone rippled in stripes through the Lhotse-Nuptse ridge. As I slowed to wait for Dorothy, an avalanche roared down between the cleft of the peaks of Ama Dablam. I stopped in respect. Many climbers have died on that mountain. On either side of the cleft, the snow clung to the steep faces in cones shaped like inverted V's.

Slowly the trail wound up through large boulders. A yak herd grazed across the river and the herder tried to move them with shrill whistles. Two baby yaks looked like furry black bears. I stopped again and a Himalayan rubythroat swooped between the scrubby bushes. Long icicles hung from a low bridge across a stream on the trail.

At 15,535 feet we reached Chhukhung. The panoramic view of the glaciers was too much for my camera. Huge walls of ice and snow clung to the face of Ama Dablam. A tiny yak was silhouetted on the moraine against a giant glacier. I felt tiny like the yak, an insignificant speck. Brightly colored prayer flags, thrust toward the mountains on a bleached pole, whipped fiercely in the wind. Dorothy and I sat without talking for a long time on the sheltered bench by the low stone lodge, feeling quite proud of ourselves and looking at the snow sculptures on the high peaks with our binoculars.

▲

May 12

Then we started down. Or up and down, really, because nothing stays level or heads in one direction in the Himalayas for very long. May 12th was election day, Nepal's first democratic plebiscite, and the trail was busy with Sherpas going to Tengboche to vote. All the activity made it not the best day for bird-watching, although we saw several white-winged grosbeaks and both the orange-flanked and white-browed bush robins. People walked several hours to get to the polling place. We saw young western-attired Sherpas, even girls in blue jeans, old men in traditional costumes including the soft boots and tunics, and women with their colorful aprons. Elderly nuns and whole families were walking. A general festive air pervaded the forests of rhododendrons. The

Barbara showing a young Sherpa boy the
Himalayan rubythroat

last part of the trail up to the monastery was dusty and steep. The rhododendrons were in full bloom, and Dorothy was especially delighted to find some bushes with deep yellow blossoms.

The saddle in which the Tengboche monastery rests is a peaceful and spectacularly beautiful place. We stayed for two nights. The monastery building, which burned a few years ago, was being rebuilt and the outer shell was finished. The panorama of mountains gives Tengboche such incredible majesty. From the high saddle we could see Everest, Lhotse-Nuptse, Tamserku, Ama Dablam, and to the west all the mountains above Namche Bazaar. Even the stream of trekkers did not reduce the dignity and peace.

The first night we sat in the lodge dining area, a spacious room with windows to the east, watching the alpen-glow on Ama Dablam as the sun faded. By now, I felt an unqualified love and respect for Dorothy, not only as a friend, but as someone who has given unselfishly to Nepal in a personal way. She told me that night about the death of her Nepali daughter.

Although Dorothy never formally adopted them, two Gurung children from the village of Siklis became her own family. The boy, Chandra, she took back to college in Colorado. He eventually got his Ph.D. and is currently head of the Annapurna Conservation Area Project. Chandra's younger sister Laxmi became Dorothy's daughter. They were so close that Laxmi once vowed she would never marry so she might tend Dorothy in her old age. Dorothy assured her no such renunciation of normal life was necessary.

Laxmi had endured severe, untreated ear infections as a small child in the village and lost eighty percent of her hearing. Dorothy took her to England, and with the help of an English friend secured medical treatment for Laxmi there. After five operations, Laxmi's hearing was effectively restored. Laxmi returned to Nepal, inspired by her medical experience to help other village children lead healthy lives. To that end she entered nurse's training.

But Laxmi became ill. When she went to the doctor she was told she had the flu. She knew the illness was more severe because she was rapidly losing weight. She returned and insisted on more tests. The test results confirmed that she had tuberculosis of the stomach. Laxmi wrote Dorothy, who was in the States at the time working on a book, a broken-hearted letter saying that she feared she would never be able to help the other children of Siklis. By the time Dorothy received the letter, Laxmi was dead.

I did not know what to say. Dorothy had turned away and her bowed head was reflected in the window toward the mountain of the mother's locket, a mountain that by now was black with night.

▲

May 13

Early in the morning we went birding, hoping to see the Impeyan pheasants that populate the forested slopes around the monastery. Although we saw some fly over low bushes in the distance, we did not get close enough to see the spectacular colors that provided me such a thrill on the Mardi Himal climb. We did add two new birds to our list, however—the chestnut-bellied rock thrush and the black-faced laughing thrush. While returning to eat breakfast in the lodge, we saw two musk deer bound down the steps of the unfinished monastery like kangaroo rabbits. They are small with large haunches and incongruous tusks on the sides of gentle little faces.

Dorothy and I decided to hike the ridge toward the Tamserku glacier and return to spend another night at Tengboche. Dorothy brought the Dalai Lama book along on our hike. A Tibetan monastery seemed a fit place to peruse the philosophy of the man who, even in exile, commands the respect of the world community as the spiritual heart and head of Tibetan Buddhism.

We climbed to a natural shelf on the ridge where a bench had been placed. The bench was surrounded by *mani* stones and prayer flags. To the south rose the face of Tamserku, its glacier shattered with awesome crevasses. To the east, through tattered prayer flags, we could see Ama Dablam, the Lhotse-Nuptse ridge, and the tip of Mt. Everest.

Dorothy and I sat on the bench, and she read aloud the Five Point Peace Plan that the Dalai Lama proposed for Tibet. He wanted Tibet to become a land where all life would be treated with dignity, where the environment and natural beauty would

Prayer flags and Ama Dablam,
the mother's locket

be protected, and where human beings would be given a chance to achieve inner peace. His beliefs—that all humans want to achieve happiness and to avoid suffering, that anger should never be returned with anger, and that even people who seem devoid of compassion have an inner core of good that is shown by their ability to respond to kindness—seem so simple, basic, and good.

Dorothy was getting cold so she decided to go down to the lodge, but I wanted to stay awhile and allow the beautiful mountains and ideas to sink through my bones and become forever part of me. I watched Dorothy hike slowly down the trail, feeling a rush of tenderness and love for this seventy-year-old woman who had climbed with me to 15,500 feet. I turned back to the east. I thought about Jim and dutifully wished he were with me. But suddenly I realized I wasn't really thinking of him at all. I was thinking of his mother.

My own mother died when I was only twenty-one, but I have been fortunate to have a genuine friendship with my husband's mother. She is a small, lively woman, a lot like Dorothy, and she loves to hike in the mountains. I've missed her sorely this year and have written long, descriptive letters to share my experience with her. She would have loved this trek with Dorothy, with all the birds, the rhododendrons, and the incredible mountains. I was positively overwhelmed with lonesomeness for her. I looked again at the mountains to the east. How my mother-in-law would love to see Mt. Everest. Suddenly my mind jumped, a physical jerk like the needle on an old record player that finally gives a hicccup and leaves the repeated phrase behind.

Not Mt. Everest, I thought. Why did I keep saying Mt. Everest? That's not the real name of the mountain. That's just a term given by male Europeans. The people who live here know what the mountain really is. The Nepali name for the highest peak in the world is *Sagarmatha*, the mother of the universe. The Tibetan name is *Chomolungma*, mother goddess of the earth. I jumped up in excitement. "Dorothy," I yelled after the tiny form. "Wait for me!" Already clouds were drifting up through slanted valleys to the west. The monsoon was coming, but Dorothy and I had almost finished our trek in the beauty of a Solu Khumbu spring.

IX

THE VIOLET SHYNESS OF
THEIR EYES

*Woman carrying basket
through herd of cattle*

1

Pokhara
June

I walked to school this morning with an unusually good view for these moisture-laden days. One edge of the clouds was lifted slightly above the mountains, like the lid of a kettle ready to break into a rolling boil. Already the valley had a steamy feel about it, too. The bony lines of ridges were much more clearly delineated on the peaks than when the winter snows fattened them. I had the sensation that someone had reached down and rearranged the model mountains to experiment with the visual effects. Machhapuchhare seemed much closer to Pokhara, with dark valleys reaching up between it and the peaks of Annapurna. Snowfields that humped smoothly on long slopes in the winter have changed to glaciated icefalls with corrugated surfaces.

It is the season of green and growing things. The *makai*, corn, has reached heights I haven't seen since the Iowa farm, and the fullness of the ears suggests a much earlier harvest than I had expected. The cannabis plants next to the Mahendra Pul bridge must measure twelve to fifteen feet. Many terraces are planted with rice, although Indu, the teacher friend I'm tutoring, tells me the main planting is a week or so away. Mangos and juicy pineapples heap in colorful piles on the fruit carts. The other day I even ate a watermelon that was quite sweet and good.

School is going well and I am pleased at the progress my students have made. The students practice their English by writing stories about their lives. Sometimes we illustrate them and make little books. Mohammad Rafik, in class six, included a particularly interesting remark about his mother today.

"I live in Pokhara. I am fourteen year old. I read in class six at Bindyabasini Barpatan school. My favorite subject is English. There are nine members in my family. Out of nine, four are my sisters and two are my brothers. I am the eldest son of my family. My father is a business man. He has opened a fancy shop in the super market. My mother's name is Aysha Khatun. She does all the work of the house. That's all."

Mohammad got a big sticker for that one. I have been giving tests to see how well individual students have mastered the material. That is almost an impossibility. It's such a circus to get each one to do her or his own work instead of sharing it with the whole row. I have to laugh. Americans here have a lot of self-righteous cant about cheating. I don't think cheating is quite the right word. In Nepal it's considered selfish not to share. Those who know are obligated to help the ones who don't know. Westerners see that sharing as some sort of moral depravity, that some are getting by with no work. On the whole, I rather like the cooperation. A lot of teaching goes on that way too, with academic students helping the ones who have more difficulty by explaining English constructions to them in Nepali. I don't complain. In fact, I play right along with blatant "cheating" if the final outcome is positive, as in the case of Durga yesterday.

Durga never used to turn a paper in because she was ashamed. She sits in the back of the class, bigger than the rest and probably older, too. Lately she has started turning in papers because she, like everyone else, wants a sticker. I would have loved to have put a sticker on one of her papers just because she turned it in, but I couldn't do it. When the papers are returned, the children look over each other's shoulder to make sure nobody who missed more than they did got a sticker. By assigning a story, I had a little more leeway. Gita gave Durga part of her story and Nirmala gave her a little more. By the time Shobha added the last part, we had a complete story (sort of), and Durga got her very own sticker. We were all so happy!

It could, after all, be considered immoral not to help people who need it. Indu gave me a good lesson in moral behavior today when we were reviewing for the TOEFL, Test of English as a Foreign Language, examination. (Because he hopes to pass it this year and get a better paying job than teaching, it's questionable whether I'm doing Nepal any favors by helping him.) Much of the exam is listening comprehension, so I read passages and questions from the practice exam book aloud. We pick out phrases he doesn't understand.

Today's practice lesson contained a little dialogue between a lawyer and client about whether "to sue" someone. Now Indu knows what a lawyer is, even though I'm told there's no tort law in Nepal. It took only a minute to get "client" straight. But "to sue" was more difficult. I tried to explain in simple terms.

"Imagine," I said, "you come to my house and you fall down the steps and break your leg. Because you fell at my house, you can sue me, and if my steps were unsafe the court will make me give you money." As I said this, I realized it made no sense, because there are very few safe stairs in Nepal.

Indu's eyes were puzzled. "Did you push me?" he asked.

"No, but it's my legal responsibility to have safe steps," I tried to explain. He shook his head.

"I would cheat you," he said. "I would not take your money."

I tried again. "If I were driving my car—" I stopped. Indu has never driven a car and I could never have made sense of American car insurance. "If your *bisee*—," I started over. (I know he has a *bisee*, because he just bought a new one a few months ago and will make water buffalo payments to the bank for years.) "If your *bisee* ran into me and hurt me—and we were in America" (the scene was ridiculous already), "I could sue you for my medical expenses."

He was incredulous. "I didn't hurt you," he remonstrated.

"But you let your *bisee* wander around." This didn't work either. In Nepal *bisee* wander around everywhere!

I thought it was hopeless, but Indu was looking at me sympathetically. "I try to understand," he said, "but I think it is hard." I agreed with him. I couldn't think of any other way to explain, so we were quiet for a minute. Then he looked at me and grinned. "I'll tell you what I think," he said. "I think the Americans have the money sickness."

2

My son Tim touched me deeply today, thanking me in a letter for teaching him to appreciate strong and independent women by the way I've lived my life. I'm humbled by his perception of my uneven struggle toward self-reliance, although I judge myself less harshly after living in Nepal. I've felt such an empathy for the women here, and seeing the blatant sexism in this society has given me a clearer picture of the deep psychological roots of problems women have at home.

In Nepal, women are clearly trapped in the role to which most societies in recorded history have relegated them. Without men they are nonentities. The degree to which they are actually degraded varies between locales and castes. The legal concept of independent rights for women is not very widespread in actual application, even when laws may be on the books.

The Brahmins and Chhetris especially practice demeaning physical customs for women, such as the wife's touching her forehead to her husband's foot. My headsir, a Brahmin, has tried to illustrate for me how things have improved for women, for he has been warned of western attitudes. He explained a phrase about women which he translated loosely, "A woman should have her head in her husband's knee." He told me that a few years ago, it was still accepted custom for a wife to show her respect for her husband by drinking the water in which she washed his feet.

But even Hem, my headsir, who tried to justify present practices as improvements from the past, didn't deny that women in Nepal were still second-class citizens at best. He said in villages girls are sometimes still married before their teens. What money there is for education and advancement is habitually reserved for males. In fact, even food itself, when choices must be made, will go to boys. My personal women friends here, except for the Gurung grandmother in my home, are exceptional for Nepali society. They are among those who have had the benefit of advanced formal schooling. But even they are controlled by men, taught to defer to men's wishes and to look down when meeting men in the road. My "enlightened" teacher friend, Indu, told me there was no question of his young wife's returning to school now that she has the baby and the duties of helping her mother-in-law.

So Nepali women are faced with a long struggle. Yet deep as my empathetic feelings go, I, for one, am not about to give them much advice on women's equality until we have things worked out a little better at home. For just a generation ago, I was taught as surely as any village Nepali girl-child that I was a second-class citizen at best and not worth very much without a man. I, like them, knew it was my duty to get married and have sons, even though my grandmother talked about preserving family names instead of religious duties to release the father's soul to the next reincarnation. Even today, many girls in America, by conscious design of religious parents or by the less conscious imitation of social custom, learn the lesson I was taught of subordination to men.

Mine was a male-dominated childhood with no men. When I was six months old, my father left. "He kissed me goodbye, even," said my mother sadly the one time she told me of it when I was home from college. "He said he would be back in a week."

But he was gone for good. He had cashed in the milk check from the cows, taken the Chevrolet that my mother had bought with her teaching money, and run away with a woman from a neighboring farm. Before he left he had deposited my mother and two babies with her mother in the big gingerbread house, and there we stayed. My mother had two dollars, a small and heavily mortgaged farm she had inherited from her own father, and a string of bad checks my father had tried to cash before he left. It was 1942 in a farming community in Iowa. She was destroyed by the disgracefulness of my father's actions. She lived out her life in quiet shyness, nurturing a large garden. We existed frugally on the rent from her land in the big house that was inhabited by my grandfather.

Only my grandfather wasn't there either as I was growing up. He had died in 1940. But he had been such a strong and domineering man that his influence was pervasive on us all. No curtains were at the windows, it was explained, because he hadn't allowed them. The big roll-top desk was never opened or used because it was full of his papers. His name was Gideon and he had been an elder in the Scotch Grove Presbyterian Church.

These two men I never met dominated my childhood. Through the women in my life I learned that men were very powerful indeed. They could destroy you, as my mother's shyness showed. And control you, as my grandmother's reverential tone conveyed when she spoke of her husband.

I also learned from my grandmother that men were much more important than women. "That's too bad," she would say when informed a neighbor's wife had just given birth to a girl. "Why do you always say that?" my mother once exploded angrily. "I just meant they needed a son to help on the farm," Grandma answered, a little miffed. But I understood, just as any Nepali girl would. "We do not celebrate the birth of a daughter," Indu explained to me when his little girl was born.

So of course I wanted to be a boy. And when I felt the first lump harden on my chest that would later prove my womanhood, I cried. At night I took the wide elastic belt that cinched my skirt at school and wore it under my pajamas, hoping it would force the chest to flatten out. What do the little girls do in Nepal, who even before the sixth class when school is no longer free, are often kept at home to do the household work? What do they think, when they, like my grandmother, are hired out at twelve to earn money for their brother's education? (I was proud to help him through the seminary, my grandma said.)

But in spite of myself I learned to be a successful girl. I learned all the lessons of the fifties. Don't run faster than the boys, don't be too smart or men won't like you, and above all, don't get yourself pregnant. Unlike Nepali society, where marriages are arranged and women continue a sisterhood of support, I learned the moral dictum that all was fair in love. That meant that no woman was truly my friend. She was a competitor. We did not help each other; we undercut each other, for our true success and worth was measured only by the men we attracted.

With my first marriage, I tried to live the myth as best I could. And for a few years I was, in a thoroughly American way, as demure as any Nepali bride with the red part in her hair, subordinating my own intellectual and professional life to my husband's career. Ironically, it was the birth of a son that brought me to the crisis point.

Truly, my first thought was that I wanted my grandmother to know I had a son, but she was dead by then. I loved the baby unconditionally from the start. And I never regretted for a minute, even for a second, that I had him, or my second son either, who was born under much more complicated circumstances. But I was miserably unhappy as a stay-at-home housewife and mother. That year my discontent drove me to read Betty Friedan's *The Feminine Mystique*. I cried with relief that I was not alone.

The time when my first marriage came undone was one of the most dramatic learning periods of my life. It took two years, really, for old myths do not die all at once. But I can look back now and pinpoint exact moments when icebergs struck the hull.

One, for example, is when I was talking with some sympathetic friends, another doctor and his wife, who were aware of our difficulties. The doctor, John, had his theory about the problem. He looked around my study, which even then was filled with books.

"Think about it, Barb," he said. "Who's read all these books?"

"I have," I answered defensively.

"See," he said, "how do you think that makes him feel? What does that do to his ego?"

I must not have answered, then, because I played and replayed that remark in my head, until one night much later (I was alone in the bed by then) I sat up in the darkness and said, "John, I don't give a damn what it does to his ego anymore." Even today I see the image that I carried in my mind, of having shed that grey confining shell and put on colorful wings to fly.

It has been at times a bumpy and uneven flight indeed. But I have been really fortunate to have my sons along. There they were, diminutive men, and I was responsible for them. In thinking through the social myths that I should impart to my sons, I learned a lot. I could see that while the myth had been monstrously unfair in the role it assigned to women, it had been monstrously unfair in the role it assigned to men as well. Then we met Jim, who wasn't interested in roles at all. So we all just bumbled along and grew together, learning to appreciate each other as people and escaping much of the gender restrictions that limit us to narrow definitions.

I've tried to extend unqualified tolerance and respect to the social customs in Nepal, even when the differences from my society have challenged personal views. But the treatment of women touches deep and personal pain. It's the sameness, not the difference here, that troubles me most. I know too well the price for accepting that distorted vision of a woman's worth. It's all I can do to keep from picking up the little girls and pointing to the butterflies. For in the violet shyness of their downcast eyes, time after time, I see my mother's face.

Nepali kitchen

Kathmandu
June

I have been hopeful about persuading the company for which my husband works to import some colorful pillow covers I sent home at Christmas. This quest led me today to the Women's Skills Development Project where the pillow covers are made.

The workshop originally was set up to train women who were destitute. Until quite recently, only the most unusual circumstances led to a woman's being economically independent here. To be without a man, if you were handicapped or in some other way unmarriageable, was to be dependent on the kindness of strangers. Another project connected with this one actually sends people to India to bring back Nepali girls who have been sold into prostitution by their fathers. I don't know if any of the workers I saw were from those ranks, but there were several with handicaps. The director, Shanti Chadha, insisted the seven girls who were deaf and mute were the best of all her workers.

Shanti means peace in Nepali. Shanti Chadha has been with the Women's Skills Development Project for several years and is very proud and protective of her "girls," as she calls the assortment of women who work in the projects.

"It was hard for me, though, when they went on strike against me during the democracy movement last year. It did hurt me, but it was good for them," she insisted loyally. "It was good they stood up for women's rights," she said.

Shanti was born a Rana. The Ranas for a long time were the ruling clan in Nepal. They are still important in politics and control considerable wealth. Shanti's father was separated from the

Shanti Chadha, the director of the Women's
Skills Development Project in Kathmandu

family under rather bizarre circumstances involving the murder of his mother. Shanti told me the story.

When the first wife of her grandfather failed to produce a son, the wife, fearful of losing control of a wealthy household, arranged that the second marriage be with a young relative whom the first wife felt secure in dominating. "It is often done that way," said Shanti. But when the young wife actually produced a boy baby and favors were bestowed on her, the older wife became quite jealous. She succeeded in having the second wife murdered when the boy was away at school. Shanti's father, when he was older and found out the truth, separated from the family and moved to Darjeeling to become an officer in the Indian army.

Shanti, one of five children, went to school in Darjeeling. I asked if it were unusual to educate the daughters. (In Nepal, less than fifteen percent of the women read and write.) "Yes," she said, "but my father said he had five fingers, some little, some big, but they were all important to his hand. He wanted us all to speak English and I was given five rupees for the first time I spoke English at home." She confided, "I was sent to a very strict school with Roman Catholic nuns. They beat us hard. It was for our own good."

By the time she was fifteen, she had passed her examinations, which coincided with the timing of her father's retirement. The family returned to Nepal. The father must have come into some of the family fortune, or at least had connections. Shanti was taken along with her mother for a visit to Nepal's ambassador to Italy, who was temporarily back in Kathmandu. The ambassador was quite impressed with the lovely young lady (she is still a striking, beautiful woman) who could speak such fluent English and seemed to know all about Rome. "The nuns described the Vatican in graphic detail; they beat it into us!" Shanti laughed. So he asked if she would like to accompany the family to Italy as a private secretary. She said yes. She didn't even ask her father's permission. "I spoke on my own," she said proudly. "My mother told everyone afterwards, 'She spoke on her own.'" In six months she was fluent in Italian and went to evening college in Rome.

After two years the ambassador was recalled in a political wrangle, and Shanti was back in Kathmandu. At the peak of the marriageable age, she wanted to work. Her father said no one would marry her if she worked, but she was young and restless. As Nepal was just opening up to the outside world, she was successful in finding employment with a travel agency. "It was," she said, "the most interesting part of my life."

She loved the work because she met people from all over the world. She related stories of them. One was of an eighty-year-old American she called Mr. John. He was taking a trip around the world, and before he came to Nepal, he engaged in such an extensive correspondence with Shanti that she felt she should go and meet him at the airport. His plane, which was supposed to arrive from India early in the morning, was delayed until four o'clock in the afternoon. This was unfortunate as he was due to fly out the next morning. As soon as she introduced herself, the old man demanded to see Mt. Everest. When Shanti tried to explain that he needed more time to see Mt. Everest, he flew into a rage, insisting he had come all the way to Nepal to see Everest, that was the only reason he had come to Nepal at all, and who was she to be telling him he couldn't see it.

They were by this time in a cab, and as they rounded the corner, the himals to the north of Kathmandu came into view. "Stop the car," Shanti shrieked, "there it is!" They jumped from the cab. "I have never seen a man so totally transformed," she said, "and he took so many pictures. But I was crying inside. I didn't want to lie, but he was such an old man." (Mt. Everest, of course, can't be seen from Kathmandu.) Later she got a letter from the man asking her to identify which peak was Everest in his enclosed photograph, and she was forced to lie again by marking a spot in the picture that was hazy and saying it hadn't shown up on the film.

But she had learned something from that episode. Many tourists cared nothing for the Nepali way of life. They cared only for seeing Mt. Everest. So she went to her boss at the travel agency and told him she wanted to charter a plane for mountain flights to see Mt. Everest. At first he scoffed at her, but she gained his permission by saying if it were not a success he could deduct the cost from her salary until it was all paid for.

This was in 1966. On the first flight she served as the guide and the hostess. "I watched how the girls stood, with their feet wide apart, you know, but I spilled my first cup of coffee anyway." The mountain flights were soon in such demand that the Royal Nepali Airlines took them over at a handsome profit. To this day, they schedule morning mountain flights from Kathmandu for those tourists who want to see Everest the easy and expensive way.

Shanti had been sent to New York for computer training for the travel agency when the marriage proposal came. She was immediately called home. I was incredulous that she would agree to an arranged marriage. "Of course," she said. "He was an officer in the Indian Army and very rich." So she went again to India to live.

She covered this part of her life very quickly. She had children and stayed home. "I was treated very well," she said. "My husband 'carried me on his head.'" For fourteen years she was very happy. Then her husband retired and they moved to Nepal to open a hotel. That was the end of her happiness. "Nepali men are all drunkards," she stated categorically. "They say to my husband, 'why do you carry your wife on your head? Women should be under your feet.'" He began to drink heavily. And he beat her and the children were afraid of him.

"I think there is a god," she said, "and he gave me this part of my life so I would understand the women I have here. You should see them when they come, ragged, battered, and tattered." Recently, her husband has developed cancer. She has had to take him to India for treatment. He is dying slowly. "I thought they would stop his drinking," she said, "but they laughed. 'Even the lion,' they told me, 'when he gets old does not drink milk, but still eats meat.'"

A few years ago during difficult times she came to work as a volunteer at the Women's Skills Project, which was in its infancy. At that time there were only twelve women in the project. When the first director left, Shanti was given the job. She decided she must turn the project into a success and do something substantial for Nepali women.

And she has. To walk through the Women's Skills Development Project is to experience hope for the women of Nepal. The women, clean and neatly dressed, sit at sewing machines surrounded by brightly colored cloth. They make dolls, pillow covers, dresses, bags, and furnishings. They cut and press and quilt. They banter back and forth across the room, and the one who was combing another's hair hopped quickly to her machine when Shanti came in with a foreigner. I was *namaste*-ed politely.

One large room, open at the sides, was used for block printing, and the large pieces of material were spread on the grass to dry in the sun. I picked out pillow covers from the brimming stock room and arranged them in the brick courtyard on the water jugs so I could take pictures to Jim.

Then I went back upstairs to bid goodbye to Shanti. The day before I'd been to a fabric fair where material producers from all over Nepal had exhibited their wares. The Women's Skills Development Project's display was by far the most professional and striking, with a handsome array of products. I asked if she had won the competition. Shanti smiled. "Oh, no," she said, "I withdrew our entry from the competition. We have won before, and some of these people have come so far. They need encouragement. I don't need rewards. I have my reward everyday when I look at the faces of my girls. I see myself in their faces."

"*Namaskaar*, Shanti," I said, raising my hands to my forehead and using the most respectful form. "I wish you peace."

At the Women's Skills Development
Project, Kathmandu

4

Pokhara
June

A few days ago I met a young woman named Roshni Gurung. She's the niece of the family downstairs, and everyone was over here for evening *daal bhaat* as Chanda's husband is home on leave from Hong Kong. Roshni is stunningly beautiful with delicate Nepali features but a western air of self assurance. Seeing her with her proud but protective father gave me a real sense that the parent-child tension that my second son Lon and I went through is not specific to one culture, even though the issues for argument seem pretty different on the surface.

Roshni's father, Deepak Gurung, is a retired officer from the Gurkha regiment of the British army, so she has lived a very different life from the majority of Nepali women I have met—or certainly any of the girls in my classes at school, even though many of them share the same last name. (It's actually a caste designation, not a surname in the western sense. Everybody's last name is Gurung in this part of town.)

Roshni grew up in a Nepali enclave on a British army base in Hong Kong. She was taught all the traditional beliefs and values of the Nepalis, but at the same time she was exposed to British culture and customs as well as the cosmopolitan scene in Hong Kong. She speaks Gurung, Nepali, Cantonese, English, and Japanese. Although her father has maintained houses in Pokhara and Kathmandu (he is very wealthy by Nepali standards with this British-scale salary), Roshni has never really lived in Nepal except for extended vacations and for two years of college at the campus in

Pokhara. Her father insisted on that. She loyally says she enjoyed becoming more acquainted with the real Nepal.

Roshni trained as an airline stewardess in Hong Kong, but now that her father has retired and moved back to Nepal, he insists that she must keep Kathmandu as her base. She took a job with a small airline that flies into Kathmandu and she works only a few days a month. She's bored and restless, and what she'd really like to do is go to the States and finish college at the University of Oregon because that's where her best friend, Archana Thapa, is studying interior design.

Roshni loves her father. That's easy to see in her sincerely solicitous remarks to him and her assurances to us that she will respect his wishes. Her mother died last year, and she obviously feels an obligation to the family. But she arrived here yesterday afternoon in blue jeans without her father, full of questions about colleges in the States. I answered what I could about Oregon and then drifted into my bedroom, leaving her with Shelby, an ardent advocate of women's rights, to plot her potential course of action.

I support wholeheartedly this young woman's quest for self-fulfillment, so it was surprising when I suddenly felt a wave of sympathy for her father. Shelby and Roshni's voices carried into the bedroom, and I had that same feeling I used to have when Lon would plot all those wild schemes on the phone upstairs when I was working on something at the dining room table. Why didn't he shut the door so I couldn't hear? I would pretend I didn't know about them, but I would worry all night.

I know how her father feels. He loves her and wants what's best for her. But his expectations for his daughter are limited by his own conditioning. He feels a tremendous pressure as a parent to turn out a socially acceptable product, and he has that intertwined with his own emotional needs. Parenting is probably a hard role to relinquish in any culture. One of the reasons I'm in Nepal this year is that I want to delineate clearly where I am headed with my life, rather than project—in the respectable guise of parenting—my unfulfilled dreams on my sons.

Both Deepak Gurung and I have designs on Roshni's future. He'd like to have her return to Pokhara, marry a nice young

Gurung, and carry on the traditions that have given meaning to his life. I, too, would like her to return because I see her as a potential piece of social dynamite for the women of Nepal. But I suspect that this truly international young woman doesn't need either of us to plot her future for her. We are much more likely to need her, with her graceful amalgamation of several cultures, to guide us through a world that we have never known.

Bride and groom, Pokhara

5

Pokhara
June

Our Gurung landlord, Bohj, who has been home on leave, left today to return to Hong Kong where he is stationed with the British Gurkha units. When I came home from school, Chanda, his wife, was sitting on the porch with the little boys, Bisal and Biswaas. The grandmother was there, too. They were resting for a minute after carrying the laundry down from the roof. It had already dried in the sun and the clouds were gathering early. Two of Chanda's sisters who live nearby came through the gate with me.

"*Bohj jannu bhayo?*" I asked. Is he gone?

"*Bhayo!*" Chanda smiled.

"*Dukha laagyo?*" Are you sad, I asked. She won't see him for another year. She just laughed.

Shelby, my housemate, and Camille, who teaches with her at the Forestry Institute, were already upstairs. Camille related a similar story. She also lives with a Gurung family in which the husband is in Hong Kong. Once, when she went up on the roof, Camille found the wife standing quietly, looking in the distance. She surmised that the woman was thinking of her husband and asked her if she were lonely. The woman looked at her in surprise, and asked, "*Kine?*" Why?

"*Shrimaan kolaagi,*" for your husband, said Camille. The woman, like Chanda, smiled.

"*Dherai didi ra bahini,*" many big and little sisters, she answered.

There must be a lesson there. Not only have I been miserably lonesome for Jim this year, I've failed to become at all close with Shelby. What's wrong with us? Almost all the western women here have chosen to live alone. I was so excited when Shelby asked me to live with her. She's only a few years older than my sons. I thought it would be rather like having a daughter without all the teenage rejection years. But it hasn't worked out that way, even though I think both of us wanted it to.

We got off to a bad start with the Gulf War. Shelby is from an extremely conservative background and takes national loyalty very seriously. I must have seemed a wild-eyed peacenik to her. But we've worked through that. We even joke about her responses to the news being the "main-stream America indicator factor" and my responses being the "radical leftist factor."

We've had moments of closeness, but much of the time I feel she's angry with me. I don't like to argue. And I guess she has a point that we can't get things right if I don't even see there's anything wrong. She quotes her mother that two women can't live in one house. I don't believe that. They do it all over the world, especially in Nepal.

I could blame the wall between us on the unresolved issues Shelby has with her own mother that she has transferred to me. But I have become an absolute master at avoiding that kind of conflict—I've only recently survived two adolescents of my own.

Or I could blame myself. I've talked so much of home this year. And that means husband and family. Perhaps for Shelby, it's seemed that I've just been hammering home that old redundant theme, that a woman, to be complete, must have a man. If so, her need to keep that dangerous thought (along with me) at bay will serve her well.

That isn't what I've meant to say to her. But I have found a new dignity this year in the part of my life that qualifies as a traditional role. And it's come from the women of Nepal. The images here are so primal and powerful. The mothers with their gleaming water jugs, the little girls with the younger siblings slung gracefully on their hips with practiced ease, the old women with their loads of firewood in tidy layers on their backs. It's as if I've felt, for the first time, the deep strength of women as the ones who have sustained their societies and carried them forward through the repetitive paroxysms of destructive violence unleashed by men. I've felt myself moving with them in a deep, quiet current that passes through generations and cultures. So I've talked of those parts of my life, too much, perhaps, for a young American woman who is trying to forge a new role under still difficult conditions within our own society.

Surely Nepali women experience all sorts of problems in getting along with each other that aren't obvious to an observer. But their general closeness is evident and it makes me feel a little ashamed that Shelby and I haven't been able to bridge our differences with a stronger bond. Neither Shelby nor I want to return to the traditional roles of women. We need to keep pushing forward together in our own society.

I hear the women laughing together downstairs, and suddenly I feel a rush of hope. Why should I project my past failed friendships on Shelby? American women were taught to distrust each other. We're working beyond that now. Our western loneliness is only a temporary cultural aberration. It's closeness—not distance—that is our natural state. That's easier to see here.

I've felt the closeness at times with Shelby and I've felt it with the women of Nepal, even in situations that used to make me feel self-conscious, like running in the morning. It would seem such a travesty—they were carrying heavy loads and I was running for exercise. Since I went through a mental crisis with the war, shedding forever the confines of national boundaries, I've lost that flush of shame when I meet them. They are real and beautiful, their curved forms against the rising sun, but in a strange way, so am I, flying along, scraggly hair and all. And we're all together, touched with the same golden light, in the early morning gaze of the sacred mountain.

6

Pokhara
June

I can hardly wait for monsoon vacation to begin so I can go back to Oregon for a brief respite. I have been staring at the walls for three days in another episode of that combination of gastro-intestinal afflictions I refer to as Brown Slime Syndrome. Maybe it's a process worthy of a patent for completing one's mid-life crisis. I feel like Vonnegut in *Slaughterhouse Five* after he and the other prisoners of war have been fed a hearty meal and promptly proceed to excrete, as he graphically puts it, everything but their brains. Then he pictures himself looking forlornly down the hole, realizing he has lost them, too.

Only what I unloaded, along with everything else in my system, was not my brains but that inner cyclone that has carried me so far from home. To be sure, the more cynical might say that the inner peace I'm feeling today is simply a gastrointestinal exhaustion as the unwelcome parasites, the storm of bacterial and amoebic infestations that have been wreaking havoc on my system for the past several days, are momentarily calmed. But I think it's more than that. In fact, I know it is, and if I were well, I should positively run to the top of the little monastery hill and raise my fist in joyous salute to the sacred mountain. As it is, I will probably settle for hobbling unsteadily into the kitchen for a cup of tea.

For the last half hour I have been listening to Shelby and Camille, who have returned from the Institute of Forestry with the story of their tribulations there. Their students are on strike demanding they have Nepali teachers instead of American teachers. Such a dilemma for us do-gooder types when we are informed we're not wanted. But now they have moved on to discuss all their sexual needs and deprivations, and having heard this lament with great regularity from most of the young western women here, I have finally tottered back to my room.

What a relief it is to get old! I'm glad for an abatement of hormonal domination. But I'm also glad I had the courage to step back from my marriage to recognize just how important sex isn't in the overall scheme of relationships. No, I won't advocate total celibacy once I return home. Enough is enough. Maybe there's no cure for sex but age. I thought that birth control would help, but as I listen to this younger generation, I realize they are as fixated on it as my generation was. Only now they have a confusing array of social signals to befuddle them in sorting out what part it should play in any meaningful relationship.

I've been lying here staring at the wall for three days. I have the big pictures Jim sent at Christmas pinned to a blue piece of material. I love them all, but the one I've kept staring at is the one I took last summer of him and the boys by the river in Yosemite. Jim and Lon had just returned from fishing. Tim and I had been sitting on the river bank in the sun, talking. Tim is kneeling by the water, the young artist in profile, studying something he is holding in his cupped hands. Lon is sitting on a boulder, looking across the river, a little restless, just ready to embark on his own. And Jim is tanned and handsome, his shirt off with just the slightest hint of a middle-age roll, a water bottle raised to his lips.

It isn't that the nights haven't been long and lonely here, because they have. But it's not sex I've missed as much as having Jim here to share the mountains. Every time I go up on the roof or climb up to the monastery, I wish that he were with me here to see the startling beauty of these peaks. I came from Iowa. I'd never climbed a mountain until the very day I met him climbing Mount St. Helens.

Jim would laugh at me now and brush off my sentimentality. And he would joke about my psychological equilibrium being directly related to my gastrointestinal system. I could assure him that, in spite of my earlier calm, I have established definitively, with repetitive trips to the *chharpi* today, that such is not the case. Without fail in Pokhara when I am sick, the water is shut off. In order to make the plumbing work, I drag pails of water up the steps from the storage tank. And the exertion sets my weakened stimulus-response mechanism into unreliable motion. I am in a cycle that is some dismal aberration of the myth of Sisyphus.

7

Pokhara
June

Today only Shuku and I went for tea. I did not ask where the others were. In Nepal it is assumed that if you are gone, you have to be, and you will return as soon as you are able. When I came back three days late after the vacation for elections because I'd been in Solu Khumbu and the planes could not fly out of Lukla, I was full of western apologies. My headsir seemed puzzled at my concern. "You were only three days gone," he said.

Shuku and I walked slowly up the hill. Shuku Pun is twenty years old and has the almond eyes I have come to associate with the ethnic groups that are closest to Tibet. Her family is from the village of Gorapani, northwest of Pokhara. Gorapani is high in the mountains on the old trade route between China and India. Shuku has seen westerners all her life because Gorapani lies on the Annapurna trekking circuit.

She hasn't been home this year, which makes her sad. Not that she doesn't have plenty of family in Pokhara, but she would like to see her father and mother, who are getting old, and her younger sisters as well. Shuku stays now at an older sister's house that is close to Byndabasini School. Her sister is married to a Ghurka soldier stationed in Hong Kong. This means there has been money for a large house. I've been to Shuku's sister's house for *bhaat* and met the various *didis*, older sisters, and *daais*, older brothers, who live there.

But Shuku couldn't go home this year because it is several days walk to Goripani. She was already juggling the vacations of her dual schedules as a teacher and a student. Besides, this year the students campaigned for their political parties in the villages during time off, which in Shuku's case was the Sun Party, the Communists.

Sometimes Shuku attends classes at the Prithi Narayan campus, the college in Pokhara. She expects to finish her B.A. degree in another year, so she is already more advanced in formal education than many of the teachers at Byndabasini School. It doesn't matter, she has assured me, that she misses most of the college classes in order to teach social studies at Byndabasini. She can get all the notes from her friends and the teachers aren't very good. If Shuku says this, it is probably true. I've noticed that even the headsir, a high caste Brahmin, asks her opinion on issues at school.

But today she was troubled. She had a paper due in her college English class and she wanted me to proofread the sentence structure. So after the *didi* had served us tea, Shuku took the paper from her bag. I'd seen her text before so I was not surprised at the difficulty of the selection. The assignment was to explicate Milton's sonnet, "On His Blindness."

I read the poem silently. It's been a joy this year to leaf through the poetry book I brought to Nepal. I've read poems I was first exposed to by well-meaning teachers in high school and realized that, at last, after successive academic degrees and decades of cultural osmosis, I can feel a personal relationship with them. If I had read Milton's sonnet at night in my room, I would have felt the poignant statement of a blind seventeenth-century devout Christian in England and appreciated the beauty and deftness of his well-turned archaic phrases. But in the *chiyaa* shop I was distracted by the reality that it was highly unlikely Shuku would share my appreciation of this poem. She stared fretfully at her paper, looking for mistakes.

I marked a few minor corrections to make the sentences flow more smoothly. Shuku writes formal, correct English, in spite of her limited oral fluency. She surely can recite the grammar rules better than I can. This paper was filled with the literary phrases that professors use, so even if Shuku hadn't made it to class, her friend had taken good notes. And Shuku, like students everywhere, had put the phrases together effectively enough that what she wrote could pass for knowledge. She didn't need my help to write this paper. She just wanted to register a complaint. She found her English class difficult and boring. She, like me, was wondering what relevance this mental exercise had to her life and to the future of Nepal.

The next class would start soon, so we paid the *didi* the three rupees for our tea and bread. I felt deeply the lack of my ability to communicate in Nepali. I wanted to ask Shuku if Milton's idea of serving god through bearing best your "mild yoke" sounded like a perpetuation of the traditional caste system her political party was trying to convince Nepal to discard. Or would it have been less boring for her to study about the blindness of Nepali children, much of it preventable with early medical intervention, than the dark world of a long-dead Englishman? Did the phrase "stand and wait," through which Milton validated his humble service to a western concept of god, ring hollow to this young revolutionary? The party with the sun for its symbol spoke of radical change. The king was the world's seventh richest man, but Nepal was ranked by the latest U.N. figures as the world's second poorest nation.

I didn't know what Shuku thought of any of this. I was merely transposing my own political ideas into her head by formulating the questions to myself. She walked beside me, her white and blue *saari* unbelievably fresh looking, while my own khaki shirt was drenched in sweat. Her dainty sandals did not scoop up the dust like my large Birkenstocks. Shuku was anxious that I would be offended that she'd found the study of my language boring.

"I will study more," she resolved. And then her face brightened. "Next Dasaii," she said, "campaign *sidio*," finished, "you with me come to meet my mother and other sisters." That was a line of poetry—in any language—that both of us could understand.

8

Where the lane on which I live joins the main road to Mahendra Pul stands a small Shiva shrine. A grated gate keeps the goats from reaching in to eat the colored rice and flower petals placed there for the god. I can tell by a sideways glance through the grate that the light is a different color inside. I never lean down to look in directly as I am shy of exhibiting such open curiosity, but I am aware of the stubby cylinder, Shiva's *lingam*, phallus, for which the offerings are brought to insure blessings for fertility and good fortune. Beside the shrine, next to the *chautarra*, the resting tree with gnarly roots, a water tap stands. This structure has none of the artistic beauty of Shiva's temple as it is set in a plain cement slab. Because of the old woman, however, this utilitarian faucet embodies for me all the symbolic magic of a sacred spring.

This tap, like all water sources in Nepal, supports a constant hum of activity even before daylight. In Mate Pani, the area of Pokhara where I live, many of the wealthy returning Gurkha soldiers bought land and built large cement-block houses with interior plumbing, but much of the population has no such amenities. A centralized water tap is to them as much a necessity as it is to the people in the hill villages. Now in the warm season, with my school on morning hours, I pass the cement platform before it is truly light. Always a line of women and children wait with water containers. People with small filled pitchers stand brushing their teeth and cleansing respiratory tracts with noisy expectorations. Saturday is the busiest day of all. I would like to sit all day by the *chautarra* simply to record the stream of humanity, but it would be impolite to be fascinated with common things. I often go that way for errands anyway, so a collage of a day's libations at this humble brass shrine is not hard to construct.

Women, who arrive at the tap singly, group in clusters to scrub the dishes and pots in the sandy mud. The clean metal gleams while they stand and talk. Both women and men carry clothes to the water in silver basins. Each garment is subjected to a rigorous ritual of kneading, pounding, and wringing through several soaping sessions. Children come in twos and threes, the smallest entirely without clothes. The oldest, or an accompanying elder, administers the shampoo. The children submit to this foamy ordeal with patient resignation.

Young women often come alone. They bathe deftly, using their *lungis*, the all-purpose wide piece of material which is sewn in a tube. These girls accomplish their body cleansing and an entire change of clothes without revealing more than a few inches of skin. No man stares and even teenage boys do not sneak covert glances, for it is part of the code of such a crowded community that private rites performed in public command their own invisible shield.

In earlier times, such complete coverings were not required of women. Once, it is said, a bevy of young cowherds were bathing naked in the river and throwing water at each other when the young god Krishna came upon them. He hid their clothes in the bushes, then called on them to rise from the water. They blushed red with shame. Then he commanded them to come from the river and one by one made love to them in the way each most desired. He bade them forever after to remain demurely dressed. And they have. Even while bathing in public.

But it is not necessarily so with old women. The first time I saw one naked to the waist washing her hair, I was shocked and asked the Nepali language trainer how this could be, in a society that required the women to be so modest. She laughed. "Old women," she replied, smiling, "do as they will."

Not that an immodest old woman bathing was a common sight. But I saw them in different places and I was once privy to a conversation where young western men stationed in villages commented derisively on the practice, so they had seen them, too.

At the center of my collage of Saturday activity at the tap would stand such an old woman. I know where she lives. She is obviously *saano chaat*, lowest caste, for the dwelling that stands along the road to Mahendra Pul, almost squashed between two taller cement block structures, is built in the old way with the orange clay and the blackened timbers. I have not seen men there. When I come home from school, she is often sitting on the narrow porch in front of her house, grinding with her pestal or stitching something by hand.

Today the woman was in the narrow strip of dirt that separates her house from the road, holding the tiniest of baby goats. I stopped and smiled, for the goat had not been there yesterday, so must have been new. She smiled in return and quickly disappeared down the dark center hallway of her house with the goat. We have a little ritual that we enact each time I stop. I stand for a moment and she comes back with another old woman who looks so much like her they surely are sisters. They both smile broadly. I have given up trying to speak as they do not answer. Perhaps my accent is so bad they do not credit my Nepali. Maybe they speak only Gurung. They could be intimidated by the surrounding shopkeepers who look on with condescending humor when I address the women. After our eyes lock, they move their hands in an awkward imitation of the western wave and I raise mine, palms together in the Nepali salute. I, too, am intimidated by the curious eyes of the shopkeepers, and simply repeat my smile and move on. But I should like to utter the most respectful greeting to them, for from the oldest of the sisters I once learned much about myself.

The lesson occurred shortly after I came to live in Pokhara, which was the loneliest time for me in Nepal. The Gulf War had just started, and I felt alienated from my own society. I lay awake much of the night, listening to the shortwave radio for news of the war. My fitful naps were punctuated by confusing snatches of dreams and memories, especially from times when my sons were small. I was just beginning to understand the ethnocentric implications of my assignment, and I walked home from school each day depressed, feeling no constructive purpose was served by my self-imposed exile from home. One Saturday, during this time, I had walked to the electrical shop in Mahendra Pul to ask the shop-keeper to fix a little reading lamp I had purchased that kept breaking with dreary repetition. When I returned, I passed the Shiva shrine and the water platform which was deserted except for the old woman.

She was singing and washing her hair. Her torso was bare to the waist, the color of dark honey with small breasts that hung like red pears. Her back was curved with age, but it glistened brown from the water and the shampoo dropped like waterfall foam on her shoulders. I was so overcome with emotion that I had to hurry down the lane, fighting the urge to cry until I gained the privacy of my house. She had unlocked a powerful memory, and when I reached my room, I lay down on my bed and relived it tearfully.

After I was left alone with the babies, I was determined not to follow the shy flight of my mother from men. I had limited resources for expensive counseling, but I read a book on the importance of dreams, and kept a pad by my bed to record them, as the author advised. One night I awoke screaming and crying. I was so upset that I could not write about the dream until morning. By then it was confused in my mind, and I recorded it wrong.

In the dream I was standing half-naked, looking in the bath-room mirror, wearing only jeans with my shirt tied around my waist. I was nervous and ashamed. Since puberty I felt shame be-cause of my small breasts. For some reason, I could not untie my shirt even though I was shivering and I knew someone was com-ing. I could hear his laughter. The way I wrote down the dream the first time was this: The man who appeared was my ex-hus-band. He was carrying a razor blade, the old steel kind with one smooth edge. As he raised the blade to my breasts, I began to scream and scream.

Months later I discovered I had remembered the dream incor-rectly. The children were with their father for the day, and I had gone with my dog to a place near Portland in the Columbia Gorge called Triple Falls. The trail curves back along a side canyon wall for a couple of miles to where the water of the creek plunges in three strands over a mossy face of rock. I know exactly where I was—the last switchback before the trail tops out to a view of the falls.

Suddenly my mind was full of the dream, and I knew I had made a mistake. The first part was the same—I stood in front of the mirror with my bare breasts. But the identity of the man who was laughing was never clear because he remained outside the door. I was the one holding the razor blade, and I was the one who began to cut at my breasts with small strokes. I understood then that I was destroying myself by accepting a distorted definition of my sexual worth. After that I began to heal.

I learned the same lesson from the old woman. Until I understood her beauty, I had feared my aging. I had thought I was losing my own sexuality, because in western society we are taught to be forever young.

"Old women do as they will." And so she did, with natural grace. Right there in view of Shiva's sacred *lingam*, she bared her breasts and stood singing in the sun.

Grandmothers at a wedding, Pokhara

THE GOLDEN HOOP WITH THE HEAVY-SIDED RIM

*Young Nepali girl with
her baby brother*

1

Pokhara
June

I ran in shorts instead of long pants this morning and felt deliciously sinful all day because of it! I'd been thinking about it ever since I started running at three-thirty a.m. in the darkness, but, oddly, even then it seemed such a cultural violation that it took me a while to get up the courage. But there's absolutely no one (human, that is) around to violate at that hour, and I've decided there's enough deference to cows around here. I planned it all last night. I dug through one of my tin trunks and found my blue running shorts where they've been buried at the bottom since I came to Nepal.

I crept quietly down the stairs and through the gate with the flashlight muffled. I walked up the rocky lane to the main road. I couldn't really focus on running until I got past Scylla and Charybdis—that's what I call the four vicious dogs on either side of the road that dare each other to attack me right after I pass the Shiva shrine. Then I began to run.

What a feeling! It was the same feeling you get when you jump in the deep end of the pool and realize it's over your head. You start treading water and your legs are surrounded by liquid buoyancy. The effect is a strange sensuous lightness as the different medium caresses you. I ran with abandon through the darkness, feeling about sixteen, as if I had stripped off all my clothes and was running naked on the beach. Of course it was still totally dark when I got home, and raining besides, so no one knew, but I've felt happy and a little wicked all day.

You'd think I'd grow up and not take such adolescent delight in things physical at my age. But I like being almost half a century old, running along smoothly. The real pleasure is feeling my body occupying only the space I need in such a crowded world, and not consuming any more calories than I absolutely must have to remain fit. I'm going to revamp my possessions and stop consuming any more than is necessary of anything, and take a serious look at how I define my needs as well. Seeing how successfully I managed with three small metal trunks all year makes me seriously ashamed of my cluttered life at home. Maybe I'll even give away some of those books.

Oh, Jim, how can I be almost fifty years old when I feel so young and excited about living and most of all about seeing you. I'm going to hold you and kiss your face and eyes, and I can't wait until we go to bed and our bodies are all tangled up and together because it seems like there's no way I can ever get close enough to you again.

And then I want to roll on the living room rug with the dogs all crazy and barking and Prune cat looking disapproving and owly. I am absolutely weak with the prospect of all that love. I have been so lonely here. All the time there has been this undercurrent of emptiness because I have walked away from what is really the substance of my life. Maybe I had to walk away for a while to understand how much it all meant to me.

I suppose the first blooming of the roses will be done, but there will be some flowers. We will go to the river with the dogs and the great blue heron will be out on the pilings. The summer evenings will be very long with the sailboats racing on the Columbia, their white sails catching the last sun like the Buddhist temple prayer flags. I find I am physically leaning toward home.

2

Kathmandu

July

I left my hotel early so I could ride my bike to the educational conference at the Himalaya Hotel. The Himalaya is out toward Patan, in Pulchowk, a good half-an-hour's ride, even when I manage to get the turns right. It isn't hard to find. The problem is that I am such a coward. I keep watching the traffic immediately around me instead of being cognizant of where I'm heading. So I take the wrong road.

This morning the traffic seemed especially congested and a steamy, polluted haze already hovered over the city. I had safely executed all the turns and was about to cross the Bagmati River, where one can look over the bridge railing to the right and see the *Juddha Ghat* with its cremation platforms, when I came upon the most distressing sight.

A cow had been killed. It must have been struck by a car in the night or early morning. It had been pushed unceremoniously to the side of the road. No one was paying attention to it now, as people in Kathmandu, like people in all big cities, are in a hurry. I pulled over to the curb and stopped my bike. I had that same sad feeling I have at home when I see graffiti scribbled on church doors. The cow was quite dead, with its eyes wide open. I rode away slowly, a taxi honking impatiently to get around me.

I arrived at the Himalaya just as the conference was starting for the second day. I guess this site was chosen for the conference as a reward for development workers stationed in villages who had been isolated from modern amenities for several months. The lobby was all marble and glass. The conference room where we met was lined with polished wood. Yesterday, when I walked in for the first time, I was embarrassed. I was aware immediately of Shashi's wide-eyed awe.

Shashi is my Nepali counterpart for teacher training. She's in an unusually high position for women in Nepali education. In fact, she was one of two women in a roomful of at least thirty Nepali men, and I thought she outclassed everyone else there. She was elegant with her unusually long eyelashes and her blue *saari*. Most of the men have given in to western emulation, and even those with the traditional *topis* on their heads wore blue jeans instead of the narrow pants with saggy seats.

Yesterday morning, after exchanging pleasantries with me in Nepali, Shashi spoke in English. She's from Pokhara, so I'd talked with her several times before. I even had a chance to watch her in action at a teacher-training workshop before her funds were cut off for the year. I'd been impressed with her workshop, which was on using practical materials in the classroom. She ran it skillfully and interacted with the other teachers with a relaxed rapport.

"Do you stay here?" Shashi asked me, looking around at the heavy chandeliers.

"Oh, no," I assured her, "I could never afford it."

"Who owns this?"

I had no idea. I was feeling most uncomfortable that she was associating this lavish hotel with me. I was remembering that she had been at Byndabasini School the day I brought my pictures from the Solu Khumbu trek with Dorothy. All the teachers had pored over the pictures, but Shashi had asked to see them a third time. She told me that none of the teachers, including her, had ever been to that part of Nepal, and probably never would be. It was too far and cost too much money.

"Maybe a foreign company owns the hotel," I suggested.

"No," she said emphatically, "I think it must be the king. It is not right that there are places like this in Nepal when there are so many poor people." She shook her head sadly. I nodded in agreement. I hoped no American company owned the hotel.

Shashi had saved me a seat this morning, too. I was glad we were close to the door. A headache above my left eye throbbed as soon as I entered the room. It was probably partly the frigid air-conditioning, but I knew it was more than that. I was dreading today.

"*Sanchai?*" Are you all right? Shashi asked.

"*Sanchai. Alikati disaa laagyo.*" I'm fine. A little intestinal trouble. I always get sick in Kathmandu. She looked a little concerned.

Yesterday was bad enough. This conference on teaching teachers how to teach was probably not an entirely bad idea, as most of the experts who had been provided by the United States government to train teachers in Nepal had never been in a classroom as teachers themselves until this year. For each American, there was a Nepali counterpart.

The workshop was being presented by one of the high-powered educational colleges in New York. Two women, about my age, who had never been to Nepal before, were running it. They were most enthusiastic presenters. They spoke very rapid English, as if their speeches had been timed and they knew exactly how long dramatic pauses could be to still finish the presentation in exactly fifty minutes. They used an overhead projector. I wondered if they had carried it with them on the plane. Whenever a new transparency was placed on the overhead projector, the Nepalis would copy the lists obediently.

The first presenter, who gave her speech yesterday, was given to bouncing across the open space in front of the chairs in dramatic sweeps. She clasped her hands and responded to all answers given, especially those by Nepalis in English, with enthusiastic, well-intentioned positive reinforcement. "May I call you Ram or is it more proper to say Ram Bahadur," she effused, putting her hand familiarly on the older man's arm.

This woman was trying to make the point in her presentation that all information to be conveyed would cluster itself naturally into four to seven steps. I think. Anyway, we were put into small discussion groups and instructed to tell the story of teaching English. Or the story of teaching science. Or whatever. So the Nepalis wrote little stories about Sita and Ram, the Nepali equivalent of Dick and Jane, that had morals about hygiene. The American development workers rolled their eyes at the obtuseness of the Nepalis. The woman then took all the lists that the groups had obediently produced on poster paper and taped them to the wall to illustrate her point about steps.

Then there had been an enormous buffet lunch. Among all the unfamiliar dishes was a gigantic mound of rice, and one of the huge soup tureens was filled with soupy *daal*. That, of course, was mostly what the Nepalis loaded on their plates, but they also took a little of everything else, especially the meat, which is a delicacy. After lunch, it became known that the meat was pork. Pork is forbidden to certain castes, and the big plates of meat had only been identified by a small card in English. There was so much grumbling that the director of the workshop apologized profusely.

The first speaker this morning was a Nepali with a Ph.D. from the University of Southern Illinois. Good, I thought, a step in the right direction. At least this man has been in Nepali schools. But he had been well trained at the University of Southern Illinois. He, too, spoke in English. He, too, used the overhead projector with a copious supply of lists, which the Nepalis obediently copied verbatim. He used words like macro and micro and went through Maslow's hierarchy to examine the question of teacher motivation.

"Some people are motivated by status," he intoned; "some people are motivated by money." We were again broken into groups to decide what we thought was the biggest problem for teacher motivation in Nepal.

I could stand it no longer. I said to Shashi, "I think the main trouble with motivation for teachers in Nepal is that they have no self-esteem. They are told they must learn from westerners how to do things the right way, so people sit around waiting for money from the West that gets skimmed off the top anyway. You ought to get rid of all the westerners. You are an ingenious people. Let the Nepalis figure out what works in education for Nepal."

"Again, say!" she commanded. I had been speaking too fast. I said it all again twice, breaking it up into small sentences. "Do you really think so?" she leaned toward me earnestly.

"Shashi, I really think so." I felt absurd tears rising. I had come to Nepal with the naive blundering so typical of my fellow citizens. I had wanted to give. Shashi smiled at me and put her hand on my arm.

When the second American lady started her presentation on assessment of learning, my hostility became a tangible thing. "Take, for example, the factor of social cohesiveness in the classroom," she said. What could she tell these people about that? To talk about social factors in Nepal one has to understand about caste and gender separation. Cohesiveness had more to do with too many bodies on one bench than with what she was addressing.

"Excuse me," I said softly to Shashi. *"Pet duhkeo."* My stomach hurts. I was glad I had said before that I was having intestinal difficulties. She nodded sympathetically. I slipped out the door. I had the same feeling I'd had at a party years before when I didn't like the substances that had appeared for entertainment. I didn't want to be in the position of telling other people I thought what they were doing was harmful. They were adults. Then, I just wanted out, so I walked out the door and all the way home to Portland across the bridge from Vancouver, Washington.

This time it was a different bridge. It crossed the Bagmati River in Nepal, and the dead cow was still there. I probably shouldn't have said what I did to Shashi. She just seemed so different there, obediently copying lists, than when I saw her giving her own workshop with Nepalis, full of easy confidence. I suppose there's some relevance to studying educational jargon like Maslow's hierarchy for a society that has discovered the importance of rushing from here to there in automobiles to make money. But they are killing cows in Kathmandu.

3

Kathmandu
July

The incredibly poignant tone of the letter I just received from my mother-in-law has me in tears. At its writing, she had just returned from visiting her brother who is terminally ill with cancer. She described her brother's suffering and the sadness of the family. Their pain is vivid and tangible in her account. Can even religion help with this long drawn-out ordeal of death? Possibly it gives an order and a dignity, a way that we can organize the pain in units that hurt no less but crest and swell in waves of prayer.

I wanted to do as she asked, to pray for Ralph not to suffer, but I had to think how I could do it sincerely since I don't have her faith. I thought of the childhood prayers I knew, although that boiled down to "The Lord's Prayer," as Presbyterians left little room for the power of comforting chants to soothe the mind. I said it a few times while thinking of Ralph. I knew it would be meaningful to my mother-in-law, but it was not coming from my heart. I wished I were still in Pokhara so I could go up to the little monastery on the hill, because I feel god knows me there. Actually, I have to turn that sentence completely inside out to get it right. I know I feel god there in a personal way. I could have walked around spinning the prayer wheels. Of course Kathmandu has both Swayumbunath and Bodhnath *stupas*, temples, with many more prayer wheels. For a Buddhist that would surely be significant, but for me the big *stupas* are simply historically and artistically impressive in the way the cathedrals of Europe are. But thinking about that little monastery gave me an idea.

A few days ago I bought a little prayer wheel made of bone

and silver for my mother-in-law. I found it in a small shop. I didn't buy it at first because it cost too much, and I'd never seen any-one use one that small. The women going up to say their prayers, whom I met every morning on my way to school, carried larger ones of metal, and I had already bought one of those from the shopkeeper I knew in Pokhara. But the more I thought of this little one, the more I wanted it for her, because it was so small and pretty. I finally went back and got it.

As I understand it, the prayer wheels, which have inscriptions *(mantras)* carved on the outside and written on the inside on a roll of rice paper, release these prayers when turned clockwise. Thousands of different *mantras* promote harmony and peace and bring out the goodness in humanity as the wheels spin. The prayer flags release them to the wind, and wheels set in streams give them to the flowing water. So here's what I did. I didn't want to take the rice paper prayer out, but I added one to it for Ralph. The prayer was about the people Ralph had loved and who loved him. Harmony, peace, the potential goodness in humanity, and love. That is all I know for sure of god. I put my paper with the other in the prayer wheel and I whirled it gently for a long time.

4

Kathmandu
July

When I first arrived in Nepal, we were taken after a few days to the village of Dandapakar on the road to Jiri. There we were housed in a compound that Swiss volunteers had built for a water project several years ago. It has apparently been inhabited by hosts of volunteer groups. The villagers were not particularly friendly, and we were urged to lock our little cement houses when we went to classes. At night, watchmen who circled the compound called to each other at intervals, which was unnerving to those of us with already troubled dreams. We were advised not to talk with villagers who might be inebriated during the Dasaii holiday. The children did not give the polite *namaste* greeting. They followed us in groups, and once a piece of gravel was lobbed and caught me on the side of the head. I did not realize until much later how unusual all of this was. I was only concerned with my own bewilderment at that point. It was in Dandapakar I first met Sapana Sharma. She was the language trainer assigned to share the small compartment where I slept.

Sapana looked like a child to me. The diminutive daintiness of the Nepali women's physique brought back all my adolescent insecurities of having attained my height before the boys my age reached puberty. Sapana was especially tiny. She told me her name, *Sapana*, meant dream in Nepali. She seemed a dark-haired elf.

"How can you be thirty-one?" I asked in astonishment, when she told me her age as we were exchanging pleasantries the first evening. "I would have thought that by guessing sixteen I was guessing old." Her laugh was a musical tinkle.

"And how can you be forty-eight?" she countered, for she had been given an information sheet about me. "If your hair were not so white, I would have said that you were thirty-one."

Sapana was patient with me. She understood that I was threatened by my slow language progress and told me the story of her struggle with Japanese. She had gone to Japan to study for a year, and did not relate well to the method in which the language was being presented. It was not until she set her own strategy of practical application that she became successful, she said. She recounted an embarrassing incident when she had asked for a book in a bakery shop. I was grateful for her tolerance.

When I slipped out in the early morning for a run, she asked if she could come along. She was the only Nepali woman I ever met who ran for exercise. She wore a long blue jogging suit. She turned back early, though, to review her lesson plans one more time. She told me how hard it was to get paid employment in Nepal. The competition for the trainer job had been fierce, and she needed to be successful. I had much to learn about the educated unemployed in developing countries.

It was unusual that she was not married. All the other women trainers were married or about to be. I didn't know at that time how unique it was for them to be employed outside the home. It wasn't until we had a training session for women only that I began to learn what marriage meant for women in Nepal. The session was set up to allow the American women to ask Nepali women what to do about nonexistent tampons and what actions to curtail to avoid being culturally offensive.

The young Americans' questions soon turned to marriage. Prabha was asked about her arranged marriage. She considered it perfectly natural, she said, and was pleased at her father's choice of a husband for her. Shasi, who was to be married in a few months but had only met her husband-to-be once, was asked for her story. She was more reluctant to talk and exhibited a little embarrassment at being singled out. But the star of the show for the Americans was Kanchan, who had gone against her father's wishes to arrange her own match, a "love marriage," while at college. A nervous giggling and tittering spread through the Nepali women. I realized Sapana was sitting a little apart from the group, her eyes on her feet.

The Americans were asking Kanchan how she was so brave to defy her father. All ended well, she said, because her husband was of the same caste so her father finally agreed to the wedding. But to make sure Kanchan's show of independence wasn't emulated, her father was already arranging her younger sister's marriage, she laughed. When I looked up again, I realized Sapana had slipped out the door.

The next morning she joined me for a run. Even in Nepal it is easier to talk of personal things when your bodies are already matched in rhythmic stride. I asked her why she had chosen not to marry, for most parents in Nepal consider it their responsibility to arrange a match while the girl is still quite young.

"Nepal isn't like America," she said. "In Nepal, if I am married, my first duty is to serve my husband and his family. My father is a most unusual man who has sent his daughters to college. I have other things I want to do in life than serve a man."

We jogged past the small Buddhist shrines and walked out the path to the cleft in the ridge where the snow-covered mountains were visible. What were these other things she wanted to do with her life, I questioned.

First, she said, she would return to Japan. Her fluency in English was reaching the point where she could soon qualify to teach that subject there. In that way she would get some capital together. Many children in Nepal lost their chance for quality life from early malnutrition. She and a friend had a plan. They would start a school, she said, for disadvantaged Nepali children. This, she thought, would be the place that she could do the most good for Nepal.

I never saw Sapana again after training ended. I heard from a mutual acquaintance that she resigned as a language trainer for the Americans after she finished the group that followed us. In a most surprising show of bluntness to foreigners, she told our mutual friend that she found her last trainees to be rude and unwilling to assume responsibility for their own learning.

I'd like to see Sapana again. I'd like to ask her how she'd feel if all the foreign governments took the money they spend to send "experts" like our group to show the Nepalis how to do things the right way, and gave it to her instead to build her school. But now that I think of it, I bet she'd tell me she didn't even need that. All of us, the parents and the teachers, who live our lives to help the children, know the answer to our success does not lie in pennies from heaven. The answer comes from within ourselves. What we need to build a better world is the dream.

Mother and child, Chhukkung

5

Pokhara
September

How fortunate I was to be in such a lovely place as Nepal to reconcile the ghosts of my Presbyterian and patriotic childhood with the present I was living and my vague vision of the future I still longed for. When the pace is slow, you can allow the kaleidescopic mental process to settle those colored bits of pain into new mosaics.

When I went back home this summer for monsoon vacation, I was anxious to see my family but almost apprehensive about returning to the United States, expecting leftover yellow ribbons and victory parades from the Gulf War. I was favorably surprised. My husband preserved our home in touchingly faithful detail. He even planted all my usual flowers in the yard and made lovely hanging baskets which reduced me to tears when I saw them. And Desert Storm had abated. The war seemed, for the most part, to exist like a morning-after alcoholic haze in people's memories.

I was tempted to stay home. The school year in Nepal fragments after monsoon vacation between extended holidays, and I knew, in reality, the students were better off with their own teachers doing the rote memory drills which they need to pass their end-of-the-year exams. The irony of my high success in improving their speaking English was that it left less time for chanting all those answers in unison, answers that are necessary for survival in this academic system. But I felt an obligation to return because I'd said I would. It is not contract law that holds you, but promises.

Jim didn't want me to leave and was very silent the last few days. He loyally insisted it was up to me, but then a strange thing happened. We were waiting on the deck for the time to go to the airport. I was pointing out to his mother the delicacy of the blue daisies and the trailing lobelia in the hanging baskets. He excused himself and went inside. When I found him, he was sobbing.

I had been, in the old way, thinking only of myself, my sense of honor, what people thought of me, what challenges I could endure to prove myself. On the plane I thought of him, his unwavering support and loyalty through this whole year and his needs now—not just the daily demands of an exhausting job while holding together a household, but his need to have me say "I love you so much that I will give back some of the freedom you have given me."

So I did. I know enough of love in all its imperfections to be profoundly grateful for what we share. I called him from Bangkok and told him I would resign and be home as soon as I could deliver my presents to my school and set up some mechanisms for on-going contact. There were tears in both our voices. After sitting up all night in the airport, I came on to Kathmandu. I resigned, then came to Pokhara to say my goodbyes.

If there's one thing Nepalis understand, it's family obligations. They were gentle and nice and a little mystified at my leaving, but not surprised. Westerners, in great abundance, with their strange, mostly superfluous suggestions for improvement, come and go here. While Nepal, blessedly, goes on being Nepal.

Yesterday morning I walked up to the little monastery behind the house. It was cloudy and hot, a yellow smudged sunrise with no himals visible to ennoble the prayer flags. I felt tired and noticed the dirtiness of the monks' robes as I followed them around to the left, spinning the prayer wheels. Nepal was just another country, filled with real and slightly soiled humanity.

But sometime during the night, the sky cleared, and this morning I sat on the roof for the last time, watching the sunrise turn the elemental images to finest art. Two children squatted in tandem by the little stream. Across the road a kneeling woman patted a clean layer of *bisee* dung and orange clay on her narrow porch. A little girl walked sleepily toward the water tap, her metal container catching the sun. As the scattered fog lifted, the terraced hills changed from muted blue to almost iridescent green. The sky deepened slightly. I lifted my eyes to the mountains. Machhapuchhare, a seamed, silver pyramid, hung suspended in the rising mist north of Pokhara. Annapurna, the goddess of plenty with her bountiful peaks, floated in a cloud of purple light. The whole scene shimmered a little, the way it looks when one has cried and tears left in the lashes form a prism of quivering color. The magic had returned.

Machhapuchhare, the sacred mountain

LIST OF PHOTOGRAPHS AND MAPS

Women traveling to Namche Bazaar, Solu Khumbu

GLOSSARY

aaimee ra ketaa-keti — women and children
Aaja bihana jaaDo thiena. — This morning it wasn't cold.
aamaa — mother
alchhi — lazy
Ama Dablam — mother's locket
Americamaa — in America
Annapurna — goddess of plenty
arko — another
aunuus — come in
baai — younger brother
bachaa ustai — like babies
bahini — younger sister
Basa! — Down!
bedeshi — foreigner
bhaat — rice
bidhaa — holiday
bihaa — wedding
Bihaa bhayo? — Are you married?
biraalo — cat
bisee — water buffalo
bistaari, bistaari — go slowly, slowly
Bohj jannu bhayo? — Is Bohj gone?
Bujhina. — I don't understand.
Bujhnu bhayo? — Did you understand?
chaumri — zup-yuks, half-cow and half-yak
chautaara — resting tree
chharpi — squat toilet
chhito — hurry
Chhori chhaina? — You have no daughters?
Chhori chhaina. — I have no daughters.
chiyaa — tea
Chiyaa janne? — Are you going to tea?
Chomolungma — Tibetan name for Everest, meaning "mother goddess of the earth"
chorten — small Buddhist shrine
daai — older brother
daal — lentils
daal bhaat — a staple meal of rice and lentils

danybaad — the closest word the Nepalis have for thank you...only for
   extraordinary actions
Dasaii — major festival occurring in the autumn
Datura — the white trumpet flower vine sacred to Shiva (a powerful
   hallucinogen)
dharma — religious duties, religion
dheari — many, very
dherai algo — very tall
dherai didi ra bahini — many big and little sisters
dherai mahango — too expensive
didi — older sister, or used when referring to the woman in charge. It is
   a term of respect.
disaa laagyo — diarrhea
doko — large cone-shaped basket
dui janna chhora — two sons
dukha — hardship, pain, sadness
Dukha laagyo? — Are you sad?
ek saya — one hundred
ekdam raamro — excellent
eklai — alone
exchen — wait a minute, one minute
gaf garne — small talk
Ghaam laageko chha. — The sun is shining.
ghat — cremation platform
hajaraamaa — grandmother
Hajur? — Pardon me, may I have your attention, yes
jaaDo — cold
jetho chhora — oldest son
Jetho chhorako naam? — What is your eldest son's name?
kaanchhi— small
kaanchho chhora — youngest son
Kaanchho chhorako naam? — What is my youngest son's name?
kakur — dog
Kati parchha? — How much?
Kati rupia? — How many rupees?
Ke? — What?
Ke kaam? — What work?
kelna — game
khannchau — eat
Kine? — Why?
kopies — notebooks
laadai kobarremaa — about the war
leka — write (command to children)
lingam — phallus
lungi — tubular piece of material worn as a skirt by women and men

maachhaa marnu — to fish (literally translated: to kill fish)
Maagne naraamro chha. — Begging is not good.
maasu — meat
Maasu kandina. — I don't eat meat.
Machhapuchhare — fish tail
makai — corn
Ma laai dinus na. — Give them to me.
Ma laai Nepaali gaarho laagyo. — I find Nepali difficult.
mandirs — temples
Mani-Rimdu — Buddhist festival
mani stones — stones carved with prayers
mantras — prayers
mero — my
Mero bichaarma, raamro bidyaarthi. — In my opinion, good students.
mero pariwaar kolaagi — for my family
Mero pariwaarmaa saat janaa chhan. — There are seven in my family.
Mero shrimaanko naam? — What is my husband's name?
Mero shrimaanko naam Jim *ho.* — My husband's name is *Jim.*
Mero umer? — How old am I?
moto — fat
My laai BBC *sunchhu.* — I listen to BBC.
naach — dance
naajik — near
namaskaar — the most respectful form of greeting
namaste — polite greeting of Nepal, meaning "I salute the god in you"
Namaste bana! — Speak the polite greeting.
naraamro — bad
naraamro bidyaarthi — bad students
Naraamro samachaar. — It was bad news.
naraamro kakur — bad dog
Nepalmaa — in Nepal
pahaad — green foothills of the Himalayas
pau roti — western type of bread
Pet duhkeo. — My stomach hurts.
pheri annus — come again
pheri leka — write again
phul — flower
prasad — food offered to the god and then passed out to the worshippers
pujaa — offerings of food for worship (usually plates of rice and flowers)
punjabis — the loose pants and tunics that the most progressive young
    Nepali women wear
raamro — good
raksi — the moonshine of Nepal
rupia — the monetary currency of Nepal
saano chaat — lowest caste

saari — dress for women that consists of several yards of lightweight cloth, wrapped and draped to form a shawl over the head or shoulder

saasu — mother-in-law

saathi — friends

sabai — all together

Sagarmatha — Nepali name for Everest, meaning "mother of the universe"

Sanchai? — Are you all right? (Is she/he all right?)

Sanchai. — I'm fine. (She/he is all right, fine.)

sapana — dream

serp — snake

shanti — peace

Sherpani — Sherpa woman

shrimaan — husband

shrimaan kolaagi — for your husband

sidio — finished

stupa — temple

sunne — listened

Taadhaa? — Is it far?

Tahaa chhaina. — I don't know.

tappai kolaagi — for you

Tapaaiko shrimaan naam ke ho? — What is your husband's name?

Thaki laagyo? — Aren't you tired?

thulo — big

thulo maanchhe — big man

thulo maanchhes — people of authority, big shots

thulo serp — big snake

Tihaar — festival honoring brothers

tika — red rice paste, used in worship

timi — you (familiar, child)

timiharu — all of you together

topis — slanted hats that many Nepali men wear

Uniharu le suthie. — They were sleeping.

ustai — the same

Uta! — Up!

wok-wok — vomiting

yeti — abominable snowman

AUTHOR'S NOTE: The Nepali language uses a different alphabet, and a great deal of latitude exists in the way phonetic renditions of the Nepali language are expressed. When there were conflicting versions, the author consulted the book used in her training, *Basic Course in Spoken Nepali* by Tika B. Karki and Chij K. Shrestha, 1988 (published by the authors).

BARBARA J. SCOT

Barbara J. Scot is an avid climber, hiker, and naturalist. She lived and taught for a year in Nepal, and has returned twice for extended visits with husband and friends. Her interest in traditional societies grew out of a trip to Egypt in 1978, and has led her to travels in Peru, Cuba, Nicaragua, and the Soviet Union. She taught social studies in high school for twenty-five years, writing extensively for class curricula. She earned a B.A. in English from Coe College in Cedar Rapids, Iowa; an M.A. in English from the University of Iowa in Iowa City; and an M.A. in history from Portland State University. A mother of two sons, she lives with her husband in Portland, Oregon.

Selected Titles from Award-Winning CALYX Books

Open Heart, by Judith Mickel Sornberger.
An elegant and genuine collection of poetry rooted in a woman's relationships with family, ancestors, and the world.
ISBN 0-934971-31-5, $9.95, paper; ISBN 0-934971-32-3, $19.95, cloth.

Raising the Tents, by Frances Payne Adler.
A personal and political volume of poetry, documenting a woman's discovery of her voice. **Finalist, 1993 WESTAF Book Awards.**
ISBN 0-934971-33-1, $9.95, paper; ISBN 0-934971-34-x, $19.95, cloth.

Killing Color, by Charlotte Watson Sherman.
These compelling, mythical short stories by a gifted storyteller delicately explore the African-American experience. **1992 GLCA New Writers Fiction Award.**
ISBN 0-934971-17-X, $9.95, paper; ISBN 0-934971-18-8, $19.95, cloth.

Mrs. Vargas and the Dead Naturalist, by Kathleen Alcalá.
Fourteen stories set in Mexico and the Southwestern U.S., written in the tradition of magical realism.
ISBN 0-934971-25-0, $9.95, paper; ISBN 0-934971-26-9, $19.95, cloth.

Ginseng and Other Tales from Manila, by Marianne Villanueva.
Poignant short stories set in the Philippines. **1992 Manila Critic's Circle National Literary Award Nominee.**
ISBN 0-934971-19-6, $9.95, paper; ISBN 0-934971-20-X, $19.95, cloth.

Black Candle, by Chitra Divakaruni.
Lyrical and honest poetry that chronicles significant moments in the lives of South Asian women. **1993 Gerbode Award.**
ISBN 0-934971-23-4, $9.95, paper; ISBN 0-934971-24-2, $19.95, cloth.

Idleness Is the Root of All Love, by Christa Reinig, translated by Ilze Mueller.
These poems by the prize-winning German poet accompany two older lesbians through a year together in love and struggle.
ISBN 0-934971-21-8, $10, paper; ISBN 0-934971-22-6, $18.95, cloth.

The Forbidden Stitch: An Asian American Women's Anthology, edited by Shirley Geok-lin Lim, et. al. **Winner of the American Book Award.**
The first Asian American women's anthology.
ISBN 0-934971-04-8, $16.95, paper; ISBN 0-934971-10-2, $32, cloth.

Colophon

Titles are typeset in Post Antiqua bold. Body text is Janson Text.
Page design, layout, and composition by ImPrint Services, Corvallis, Oregon.